DATE DUE

11/13/9			

DATE DUE

11/13/9			

EXTRAORDINARY EVIL

Also by Barbara Coloroso

kids are worth it!

Parenting through Crisis

Parenting Wit and Wisdom from Barbara Coloroso

The Bully, the Bullied, and the Bystander

Just Because It's Not Wrong Doesn't Make It Right

EXTRAORDINARY
EVIL
A SHORT WALK
TO GENOCIDE

BARBARA COLOROSO

NATION BOOKS
NEW YORK
WWW.NATIONBOOKS.ORG

Published by
Nation Books
A Member of the Perseus Books Group
116 East 16th Street, 8th Floor
New York, NY 10003

Nation Books is a co-publishing venture of the Nation
Institute and the Perseus Books Group

Books published by Nation Books are available at
special discounts for bulk purchases in the United States
by corporations, institutions, and other organizations.
For more information, please contact the Special
Markets Department at the Perseus Books Group,
2300 Chestnut Street, Suite 200, Philadelphia, PA
19103, or call (800) 255–1514, or e-mail
special.markets@perseusbooks.com.

Library of Congress Cataloging-in-Publication Data
is available

ISBN–10: 1–56858–371-0
ISBN–13: 978–1–56858–371-6

10 9 8 7 6 5 4 3 2 1

It is not the fuction of history to drum ethical lessons into our brains. The only thing one can learn from history is that actions have consequences and that certain choices once made are irretrievable.

—GERDA LERNER, *THE CREATION OF PATRIARCHY*

*In honor of the women and men and young girls and boys
who suffered horrors beyond the imagination
of most of us and survived to deny
the* genocidaires *a victory*

I am a survivor of a concentration camp. My eyes saw what no man should witness: Gas chambers built by learned engineers, children poisoned by educated physicians, infants killed by trained nurses, women and babies shot and buried by High School and College Graduates. So I am suspicious of education.

My request is: Help your students to become human. Your efforts must never produce learned monsters, skilled psychopaths, educated Eichmanns. Reading, writing, and arithmetic are important only if they serve to make our children more human.

—CHAIM GINOTT, 1972

Contents

Introduction:
A Wall in Kigali

Nothing rips more at the common fabric of
humanity than genocide—and the only way to
assert our own humanity is to stand up to it.
　　　　—NICHOLAS D. KRISTOF, *NEW YORK TIMES*

In Kigali, Rwanda, there is a memorial on the grounds
where ten Belgian soldiers were murdered in the first days
of the 1994 genocide. In one room of the bullet-riddled
building is an exhibit representing genocides from around
the world. I walked from one picture to another, staring at
humankind's ability to destroy, in extraordinarily cruel and
vicious ways, our brothers and sisters, fathers and mothers,
neighbors, and other kin. At the end of the exhibit was a
poster with the word "Genocide" at the top and cracked
human skulls at the bottom. In between was a listing of
thirteen episodes of crimes against humanity, ranked
according to the number of people killed.

1. North America (1492–) 15,000,000 people
2. South America (1500–) 14,000,000 people

3. Holocaust in Europe (1933–1945) 6,000,000 people
4. Cambodia (1975) 2,000,000 people
5. Pakistan (1971) 1,500,000 people
6. Armenia (1915–1918) 1,400,000 people
7. Rwanda (1994) 1,000,000 people
8. Former Yugoslavia (1991–1999) 800,000
9. Uganda (1971–1979) 300,000
10. Manchuria (1930) 200,000
11. Iraq (1980–1988) 100,000
12. South Africa (1902) 30,000
13. Australia (1824) 10,000

Below this poster, scribbled on the wall, was the following:

14. *Sudan 200,000 and counting

The list did not include the Herero and Namaqua in South West Africa (Namibia) slaughtered by the Germans from 1904 to 1907, the Roma and Sinti and other "undesirables" killed by the Nazis and their co-conspirators from 1933 to 1945, the slaughter of the Chechen Ingush, the Crimean Tartars, and the Volga Germans by the Soviets during World War II, the half million Communists and Chinese massacred in Indonesia in 1965, the close to 1 million Ibo killed in fighting and an enforced famine by the Nigerian Federal Army and the government that supported it against the newly formed country of Biafra in 1967, the 3 million dead and the 250,000 women and girls raped in Bangladesh in 1971, the 1972–73 slaughter by the predominantly Tutsi army of

200,000 Hutu in Burundi under the Micombero government, the mass murder, starvation, and death by torture of 200,000 people from East Timor by Indonesian military forces in the mid-1970s, the "disappearance" of 2,600 during General Augusto Pinochet's reign of terror in Chile from 1973 through 1990, the gassing of the Kurds in northern Iraq by Saddam Hussein's regime in 1988, or other mass murders and "disappearances" of whole groups of peoples throughout the world during the last century. In fact, in the twentieth century, genocide and mass murders—all crimes against humanity—have killed an estimated 60 million men, women, and children—more than were killed in battlefields in all the wars from 1900 to 2000.

And the twenty-first century is not off to such a great start. Sudan's decades-long crisis has killed more than 2.5 million from a population of 41 million and displaced another 4.5 million, with more deaths to come from disease and hunger. In spite of the explicit naming of this event as a genocide by the international community, and the arrival of an ill-equipped, inadequately trained, and understaffed African-led force to "keep the peace," the Sudanese government refuses to rein in its very real, supposedly nonexistent militias, and is balking at accepting a properly mandated, fully equipped United Nations force. As if the sovereignty of a state is sacrosanct, regardless of its actions, the United Nations is seeking permission from those very same people who are instigating and perpetrating the genocide to *allow* UN troops to defend vulnerable and desperate civilians in Darfur. The first genocide of the twenty-first century seems to be following a script eerily similar to that of the last genocide of the twentieth century.

Regardless of who was or was not included on the list, the statistics give only the mathematics of genocide and mass murders in absolute terms—the ranking of crimes against humanity by the number of people killed, ignoring each one's uniqueness and its singular attributes, the percentage or proportion of the targeted population it left dead. The list does not allow for comparisons of genocides other than by their sheer "final tally" numbers.

It was not the poster with the numerical rankings in the memorial that took my breath away. It was the individual pictures and stories surrounding it that made real the horror behind these statistics. A child pleading with the Interahamwe to spare his life and he will promise not to be a Tutsi any more. A young woman in a field telling of "bleeding from a wound that will never ever scar over. Coming out of my hiding place, I saw that they had caught Maman. She lay floating in the mud.... Papa and Godmother and the rest of the family were killed shortly afterwards.... Papa was run through by a Hutu neighbor who danced and sang over him.... I saw many people cut beside me, all the time I fought down a tenacious fear, truly an all too great terror. I overcame it, but I'm not saying it has left me forever." Twelve-year-old Cassius speaking of the middle of the afternoon when the Interahamwe burned little children before the front door: "With my own eyes, I saw them writhing from the burns completely alive, truly. There was a strong smell of meat, and of petrol." And then there were the pictures of beautiful children with a one-line caption under each of their names: Fidele (9 years), shot in the head; Patrick (5 years), hacked by machete; Ariane (4 years), stabbed in her eyes and head; Thierry (9 months), hacked by machete with his mother; Aurore (2 years), burned alive in Gikondo Chapel; Hubert (2 years), shot dead; Uwamwezi (2 years), grenade thrown in the shower.

I was on this trip to Rwanda in the summer of 2005 to work with children orphaned in 1994, children who had managed to survive the genocide that many of their peers and families did not. On my first full day in the capital city, Kigali, I met twenty-one-year-old Jean Paul. Jean Paul would not go into the National Genocide Memorial Museum with us. Instead, at the gateway arch of the complex, he stood as a lone sentry guarding simultaneously the graveyard in front of him and the hauntingly beautiful hills behind.

In April 1994, the Hutu Power extremists in the government of Rwanda called upon the Hutu majority to kill everyone in the Tutsi minority along with any "moderate" Hutus who in any way opposed Hutu Power or were sympathetic to and thus accomplices of the Tutsis. When he was only eleven, Jean Paul, his two sisters, and their parents fled to the large church compound in Nyarabuye, seeking what General Roméo Dallaire has described as "God's protection [that] ended instead in the arms of Lucifer." With Jean Paul's sisters and mother fleeing ahead of them, Jean Paul and his father arrived at the church, hid together in the bushes, and witnessed his mother try in vain

to protect his sisters as they were felled by machetes. Jean
Paul's father in turn tried to protect his only son as the *genocidaires* came after them. Jean Paul saw his father killed in
front of him, and he himself was slashed four times by the
sharp blades. He fled into a nave and stood frozen in fear as
he watched the murderers finish their work of "killing the
cockroaches" with machetes and *masu,* their nail-studded
clubs. Terrified, Jean Paul fled alone into the hills.

In one hundred days, almost one million men, women,
and children were murdered by their neighbors, school-
mates, colleagues, relatives, and supposed friends. An
estimated 400,000 of the dead were children, and 95,000
more were orphaned. Children were brutally massacred—
killed in their homes, in schools, and in hospitals. Newborn
babies were murdered in the maternity clinics where they
were born. More babies were stolen from their mothers,
only to be butchered. Tutsi mothers were forced to kill their
own infant sons. Thousands of children were drowned,
burned, buried alive, thrown down toilets while wounded
and left for dead. The human rights organization African
Rights detailed the fate of these children in their treatise
Rwanda: Death, Despair and Defiance. The text describes
how some parents, standing on a riverbank,

> threw their children into the water to spare them the
> death by machete. It was in the words of one survivor,
> "a last gesture of love" … Others, strapped to the
> backs of their mothers, drowned when their mothers
> were forced to jump into rivers.

Many of the young girls who survived were victimized in different ways: abducted, raped, impregnated.

A nurse, Sister Marianne, who herself hid in the basement of a convent for days, was asked to help in the intensive care unit in one of the hospitals in Kigali during the genocide. After witnessing "the most sickening sights imaginable," including her own little niece—the sole survivor of her family of nine—with deep machete cuts to her head, Sister Marianne kept asking herself: "What kind of human beings can do this to children?"

I, too, asked that question over and over again as I witnessed the battered and mutilated orphans who still managed to get up each morning and face a new day often filled with uncertainty, poverty, and pain in a moral world that has been "turned on its head."

Contempt (Bullying) to Hate Crime (Criminal Bullying) to Genocide (Extraordinary Evil)

Real ideas must as a rule be simplified to the level of a child's understanding if they are to arouse the masses to historic actions. A childish illusion, fixed in the minds of all children born in a certain decade and hammered home for four years, can easily reappear as a deadly serious political ideology twenty years later.

—SEBASTIAN HAFFNER, *DEFYING HITLER: A MEMOIR*

As a concept and as a fact, historical and present-day, the slaughter of whole groups of people by other seemingly ordinary human beings has been a subject of enduring, increasingly urgent interest to me. My introduction was a copy of Elie Wiesel's *Night*, which I picked up from a large bin of used books, marked up and well worn, while passing through an airport in the early 1970s, on my way to a conference to give a speech. I had a basic knowledge of the genocide of the Jews and was familiar with Wiesel's writings, but nothing prepared me for his terrifying personal account of the horrors of the Auschwitz concentration camp, where he witnessed, as the book's publisher describes it, "the death of his family ... the death of his innocence ... and the death of his God."

Haunted by Wiesel's story, I began my own study of what Hannah Arendt has described as the "banality of evil." In particular, I wanted to explore what in our dispositions and situations could possibly allow such evil to be perpetrated by ordinary people, without shame, compassion, or mercy. Yehuda Bauer argues that the horror that genocide evokes in us "doesn't remove it from the realm of human nature or human comprehension; it makes it a disturbing fact of human nature, not necessarily a metaphysical mystery."

As an educator, I found my "side study" of genocide—this "disturbing fact of human nature"—seeping into my lectures and eventually into my writings. On my lecture tours, I extended stays in Germany, France, Belgium, North and South America, Australia, and New Zealand to visit genocide museums, memorials both formal and makeshift, mass graves marked unceremoniously with wooden plaques, landmarks of slaughter around the world. I sought out movies and surfed the Internet for the history that was omitted from my high school and university courses. I listened to survivors—Guatemalan women who spoke about their spouses, sons and daughters, brothers and sisters, fathers and mothers who simply "disappeared" (a shadow reference to the even larger number of "disappeared" in Argentina); young Maori boys in New Zealand who told stories of being targeted by their peers for ridicule and harassment—and visited the places in Australia depicted in *Rabbit-Proof Fence*, a movie that exposed the dark underbelly of government policies concerning indigenous peoples of the outback.

In the mid-1990s, seeing an article in my hometown *Denver Post* about a fifteen-year-old Serbian war refugee struggling to attend high school classes while holding down a full-time job to support himself and his mother, I called the Ecumenical Refugee Service to see if we, as a family, could sponsor Mladin and his mom, Ljubicá. I was told a church was sponsoring them (partially true) but that he had a Muslim friend, Damir, whom he had met in the United Nations refugee camp in Croatia. Would our family be willing to sponsor him, his sister, Aida, and their parents, Atif and Slavicá? And then came another friend, Aleksander, and his three sisters, Angelina, Anita, and Aleksandra, and their parents, Miodrag and Andelka, and finally Atif's twin brothers and their families.

No longer merely numbers from the war and crimes against humanity in the former Yugoslavia, these families shared with us their personal stories: Mladin forced onto the Serbian front lines as fodder for incoming bullets; Atif hiding in a closet as Slobodan Milosevic's henchmen made their way methodically through Banja Luka, killing each and every Muslim male they found. Atif then fleeing with his family to a UN refugee camp; Miodrag refusing to bear arms, his family hiding in walls and small rooms, dodging bombs and bullets; both Damir and Aleksander assuming different names so as to hide their ethnic identity, an identity that had been insignificant up until the death of Tito.

Then, in 2005, I was invited to the University of Rwanda in Butare to lecture on my latest book, *The Bully, the Bullied, and the Bystander*. In 1994, many senior academics at this university had participated actively in the genocide, betraying and encouraging the murder of their Tutsi colleagues and students, manning roadblocks, and taking killers to the various massacre sites. Eleven years later, the campus bore no visible scars, but there was an undeniable tension still present. Rather than give a talk only about school yard bullying, I used the opportunity to demonstrate that the concept of genocide in general, and the Rwandan genocide in particular, are macrocosms of the drama known as bullying—a theme alluded to but not fully addressed or developed in my book on childhood bullying. I suggested in that lecture that genocide is not an unimaginable horror—that, on the contrary, every genocide throughout human history has been thoroughly imagined, meticulously planned, and brutally executed.

That said, I must agree with Claude Lanzmann, the maker of the film *Shoah*, who is adamant about the "obscenity of the very project of understanding [genocide]." I don't think it is possible to fully understand such evil, nor would I want to. That should not prevent us from studying it. Genocide is not outside the realm of ordinary human behavior. At the same time it is not normal, natural, or necessary. It is the most extreme form of bullying—a far too common behavior that is learned in childhood and rooted in contempt for another human being who has been deemed to be, by the bully and his or her accomplices, worthless, inferior, and undeserving of respect. The progression from taunting to hacking a child to death is not a great leap but actually a short walk. To begin to examine genocide is to first examine those steps.

The day before I gave that lecture, an administrator at a prestigious girls' school in Kigali shared with me an incident that had occurred at the end of the 2005 school year—eleven years after the genocide. A fifteen-year-old girl had found under her pillow a note from a classmate to the effect that the job of "cutting the trees was not yet completed" and that her long neck would soon have a necklace of machete cuts. Step one.

The pain of a "moral world turned on its head" does not begin with the machete cuts of the Hutu Power, the gas chambers of the Nazis, the death marches of the Young Turks. The tragedy of genocide has many rehearsals that weaken moral inhibitions against violence, publicity that spreads bigotry and intolerance, a backdrop that establishes the climate, ominous sounds that signal the beginning and the end, scripts that heighten the tension and fuel the contempt, six scenes that seal the victims' fate, a slew of character actors, and an international audience that either fails to hinder or actually helps to energize the performance of acts of extraordinary evil by ordinary people.

This summer I returned to Rwanda with my twenty-eight-year-old son, Joseph, to work once again with the Tumurere Foundation. The Tumurere Foundation in Kigali has been a refuge in the living hell that was created by the genocide and its aftermath for children orphaned in the slaughter. The men and women—all survivors themselves—with little funding and even less international concern, work tirelessly to create stable family lives and provide funding for education for but a small number of those whose families were ripped apart. Their work is a testament to the potential of caring deeply, sharing generously, and helping willingly—three of the known antidotes to the virulent agents of hating, hoarding, and harming that tear apart the fabric of our humanity.

EXTRAORDINARY EVIL is a summation up to this point of my almost-thirty-year study of genocide, historical and present-day. It begins with an examination of the word *genocide*, a new word for an ancient practice that, in the twentieth century, morphed into something far more menacing and destructive. Looking first at the occurrences of genocide as a historical phenomenon, in this book I posit the underlying conditions necessary for genocide to take place, and survey three genocides of the twentieth century through the lens of those conditions. *Extraordinary Evil* examines the accepted wisdom concerning genocide and the myths about it, both common and uncommon. It questions those myths, and offers alternative ways of understanding the human phenomenon of genocide. It looks at those who have stood against it, the resisters, defenders, and witnesses who defied all to protect and speak for those targeted and felled by genocide. And finally, it looks at the aftermath of genocide, both within the affected nation and without. What are the long-term effects on a nation, and on the fabric of the world at large, in the aftermath of genocide?

From the perspective, and often through the prism, of their own disciplines, historians, social scientists, physicians, and genocide scholars have written countless articles and books about genocide in general and each of these tragedies in particular. Human rights groups have collected data and put a name and a human face to the perpetrators, the targets, the bystanders, and the defenders, the resisters, and the witnesses. Fiction writers, such as Franz Werfel *(The Forty Days of Musa Dagh)*, have told stories that, as Salman Rushdie has said, are "lies that tell the truth" about life. Filmmakers like Steven Spielberg have given us such works as *Schindler's List*, depicting the horror and the humanity. Artists have memorialized the agony in pictures, in sculptures, in paintings, and in monuments. People who survived the death marches, the death camps, and the deadly blows of machetes have recorded their memoirs, written novels and university texts, issued warnings, and spoken out against such injustices as only those who have lived through the horror of genocide can.

I write *Extraordinary Evil* as an educator, a parent, and a former nun. All three of these influence and color this text.

> Genocides are deadly to the victims; they are also events whose corrupting character travels deep into the population. The successors to the societies that have been consumed by mass violence cannot escape the legacy; they remain overburdened by the past, precisely because of the participatory nature of genocide in the modern era.
>
> —ERIC D. WEITZ, *A CENTURY OF GENOCIDE: UTOPIAS OF RACE AND NATION*

Chapter 1

Genocide: A Definition

Quite obviously, if humanity is to develop sound
conventions and effective warning systems in
order to stave off genocide, then scholars,
activists, governmental officials, and others need
to come to a consensus in regard to that which
does and does not constitute genocide.

—SAMUEL TOTTEN, "WRESTLING WITH
THE DEFINITION OF 'GENOCIDE'"

In his BBC radio broadcast of August 1941, British Prime
Minister Winston Churchill said, "The whole of Europe
has been wrecked and trampled down by the mechanical
weapons and barbaric fury of the Nazis.... As his armies
advance, whole districts are exterminated.... We are in the
presence of a crime without a name."

Churchill was accurate in describing the barbaric fury of
the Nazis, but the extermination of whole districts that he
referred to had already been named; under international
law, this was a "war crime." Still, lurking in the midst of so
much devastation was the actual "crime without a name,"
that is, the planned, deliberate destruction of a people. This

crime would become known as "genocide," a word derived from the ancient Greek word *genos* (race, kin, or tribe) and the Latin *cide*, from *caedere* (to cut, to kill). The eminent Polish Jewish scholar, author, and lawyer Raphäel Lemkin coined the term in 1943, and it appeared in print for the first time in 1944 in his book *Axis Rule in Occupied Europe: Laws of Occupation, Analysis of Government, Proposals for Redress*. This work was a continuation of Lemkin's 1933 Madrid Proposal, a paper presented to his European legal colleagues in which he drew attention to the Ottoman slaughter of the Armenians, and it offered an analysis of German occupation policies in Europe, including Hitler's ascent to power. Lemkin argued that if it could happen there (Ottoman Empire), it could happen here. It happened once; it would happen again. Impunity for mass murderers had to end. Retribution had to be legalized. The attempt to wipe out groups like the Armenians, Lemkin argued, would have to be codified as an international crime that could be punished anywhere. Up to that point, no international convention existed to cover crimes perpetrated by a state (or party in power) against its own people.

As a League of Nations specialist and a member of the International Bureau for Unification of Criminal Law, Lemkin launched a personal drive to declare it a crime to systematically destroy a group targeted for its national, ethnic, racial, or religious makeup, adding that such a crime was so big that nothing less than declaring it an international offense would be adequate. In the Madrid Proposal, Lemkin suggested the creation of a multilateral convention making the extermination of human groups an international crime, since such crimes threatened the interests of the entire international community. Such "Acts of Barbarity and Vandalism," as he called them, were general dangers—crimes of significance to more than one nation. Speaking of some offenses as concerning "attacks on individual rights ... while other offenses relate to the relations between the individual and the collectivity, as well as the relationship between two or more collectivities," Lemkin went on to describe "Acts of Barbarity and Vandalism" as a deadly combination of these two elements. These acts were systematic and purposeful, not spontaneous or random.

In *Axis Rule*, Lemkin further developed the concept of such a crime, now calling it "genocide" and noting, "While society sought protection against individual crimes, or rather crimes directed at individuals, there has been no serious endeavor to prevent and punish the murder and destruction of millions." Citing the 1915 annihilation of the Armenians as a seminal example, he commented, "Genocide is not only a crime against the rules of war, but also a crime against humanity." Lemkin insisted that "to treat genocide as a crime that only concerns an individual nation makes no sense because by its very nature the author is either the state itself or powerful groups backed by the state ... by its legal, moral and human nature, genocide must be regarded as an international crime." He went on to write that genocide has two phases: one, the destruction of the national pattern of the oppressed group; the other, the imposition of the national pattern of the oppressor.

In their book *The History and Sociology of Genocide*, Frank Chalk and Kurt Jonassohn describe these phases:

> Adding shading to an already sinister picture, no sooner had the Armenian population been physically removed or liquidated and replaced by a Turkish or Kurdish one, than all symbolic, cultural traces of the former inhabitants such as churches and place names were destroyed and eradicated. It was as if the Committee of Union and Progress (CUP) had wanted to obliterate even the memory of Armenian existence.

Reflecting on the evolution of the concept of such a crime against humanity, Lemkin wrote in his memoir, *Totally Unofficial Man*, that following the bombing of Warsaw in 1939, he "knew that this was more than war, that this was the beginning of genocide on a large scale." In the United States, the actions of Hitler were framed as the Nazis waging war against European armies. Lemkin pleaded with officials to see that Hitler was systematically and ruthlessly wiping out the Jews. His pleadings were met with indifference and incredulity.

Two years after the publication of *Axis Rule*, on December 11, 1946, the General Assembly of the United Nations passed an initial resolution that stated in part:

> Genocide is a denial of the right of existence of entire human groups, as homicide is the denial of the right

to lives of individual human beings.... Many instances of such crimes of genocide have occurred, when racial, religious, political, and other groups have been destroyed entirely or in part....

The General Assembly Therefore, Affirms that genocide is a crime under international law which the civilized world condemns, for the commission of which principals and accomplices—whether private individuals, public officials, or statesmen, and whether the crime is committed on religious, racial, political or any other grounds—are punishable.

Two more years later, on December 9, 1948, after much heated discussion, serious disagreement, and ample political compromise, the United Nations General Assembly adopted "Resolution 260 (III) A: The Convention on the Prevention and Punishment of the Crime of Genocide (UNCG)." Genocide was defined as "acts committed with intention to destroy in whole or in part, a national, ethnical, racial or religious group, as such:

a. Killing members of the group;
b. Causing serious bodily or mental harm to members of the group;
c. Deliberately inflicting on the group conditions of life calculated to bring about its physical destruction in whole or in part;
d. Imposing measures intended to prevent births within the group;

e. Forcibly transferring children of the group to another group.

Article III of the Convention lists the following acts as punishable:

a. Genocide;
b. Conspiracy to commit genocide;
c. Direct and public incitement to commit genocide;
d. Attempt to commit genocide;
e. Complicity in genocide.

The final draft both tightened the definition and expanded it. This definition did not include political, social, or gender groups (which would later have enabled an indictment of genocide in the case of nearly 500,000 "Communists" killed in Indonesia in 1965, and in the case of the murders of city-dwellers and the educated elite by the Khmer Rouge in Cambodia in the 1970s). The Convention also narrowed Lemkin's original formulation, which had included ethnocide (the destruction of a culture, such as the forced assimilation of a group by preventing the use of its language) and ethnic cleansing (the forced removal of a targeted population). Ethnic cleansing and genocide are not one and the same, but they often go hand in hand. Mass movement of large populations is often deadly, and when mass movement is not feasible or possible, the intention inherent in ethnic cleansing can quickly and easily morph cleansing into extermination.

However, the draft did list "national" and "ethnic" groups specifically, rather than leaving them to fall under the category of "other." And through the use of the phrase "in part," the definition also allowed for the consideration of such genocides as those committed against indigenous peoples of North and South America.

Over the past sixty years there have been many discussions, debates, and serious disagreements concerning the wording of the United Nations Convention on Genocide: it is argued that the definition is too inclusive, too exclusive, too narrow, too broad; that its definition of "intent" is too easily misunderstood and often interpreted incorrectly; that the phrase "in whole or in part" is too ambiguous to be of much use practically and legally. Some legal scholars, genocide researchers, psychologists, and social scientists suggest that a complete overhaul of the definition is needed, to make it more "analytically rigorous" (as suggested by historian Frank Chalk and sociologist Kurt Jonassohn); more humane, so as to protect all targeted groups (as suggested by psychologist Israel Charny); and more inclusive (as suggested by Dutch law professor Pieter N. Drost), by defining genocide as "the deliberate destruction of physical life of individual human beings by reason of any human collectivity as such."

The Convention entered into force on January 12, 1951. To date, more than 137 nations have ratified it and more than 70 nations have made provisions for the punishment of genocide in their domestic law. More than 50 nations have not ratified it. With all its shortcomings and weaknesses, the UNCG definition laid the necessary groundwork for framing the three main issues of the "crime with no name": intentionality of the perpetrators, the fate of the defined targeted groups, and physical annihilation as the goal or potential result.

PROSECUTING THE CRIME

In 1945, the Allies convened the International Military Tribunal at Nürnberg, and other trials throughout Europe, for the purpose of holding Nazi war criminals and collaborators accountable for their "crimes against the peace of the world." This term was introduced by the Allies in World War I to label the actions of the Turks against the Armenians, when, between 1915 and 1917, under the nationalist government of the Young Turks, the Turks drove more than a million Armenians in the Ottoman Empire from their homes and annihilated them. Lemkin served as an advisor to U.S. Justice Robert Jackson at the Nürnberg Tribunal and pushed to have the Nazi war criminals found guilty of genocide. None was, even though the French prosecutor at the trials, François de Menthon, described their crimes as not "war crimes" or "crimes against peace" but the very worst of crimes, "crimes against the status of being human." Jews were killed simply because they were Jews. Those convicted were punished only for crimes committed in connection with "the war of aggression," i.e., aggressive war or the violation of another state's sovereignty. As much as Lemkin pleaded to have the charge of genocide included in the convictions, the Nazi defendants were instead convicted of "crimes against peace," "war crimes," and "crimes against humanity," all with reference to deeds committed outside Germany's borders. The charge of genocide was included in some indictments in the trials, but no verdict was leveled on this charge for any of the defendants. Similar judgments on charges of "crimes against the peace of the world" were rendered at the Tokyo War Crimes Tribunal that convened at the conclusion of World War II.

The same myopic vision that caused the United States to see the actions of Hitler and his henchmen as only the waging of *war* against European armies was what caused the Tribunals to fail to recognize the *genocide* of the Jews as a crime separate and worlds apart from the crimes for which the verdicts were rendered. Sixty years later, during the genocide in Rwanda, a similar failure of vision would distort how the international community saw the extermination of the Tutsis. In his book *Eyewitness to a Genocide: The United Nations and Rwanda*, professor of political science Michael Barnett wrote:

> The [United Nations] Secretariat's mentality, how it was organized to think, and the social optics it donned, shaped how it saw and acted upon Rwanda, making it difficult for it to see the warning signs of genocide and leading it to interpret the violence against civilians as nothing other than an awful feature of civil war.

It was only after nearly one million human beings were hacked to death in less than one hundred days that the international community would see clearly—far too late— what had been right in front of them: the most grievous crime against humanity, another genocide.

GENOCIDE CONVICTIONS

The human desire to "right wrongs" is as old as recorded history. We pursue justice because we wish to be vindicated and, more importantly, to have what we have lost returned. Yet it seldom is.

—MY NEIGHBOR, MY ENEMY: JUSTICE AND COMMUNITY IN THE AFTERMATH OF MASS ATROCITY

The Genocide Convention of December 9, 1948, along with the Universal Declaration of Human Rights that was adopted a day later, provided the legal basis for the writ of two international tribunals convened by the United Nations Security Council in the 1990s, one in the Hague and concerned with events in the former Yugoslavia, the other in Arusha for crimes in Rwanda. It is in its application by these courts that the UN's definition of genocide is finally gaining force in the international community—some sixty years after the original convention.

On September 2, 1998, at the UN tribunal for Rwanda in Arusha, Tanzania, Judge Laity Kama pronounced the first ever verdict in a UN tribunal for the crime Lemkin named: "The accused, Jean-Paul Akayesu, you are declared guilty of genocide."

It must be noted that there were also genocide trials conducted in Rwanda. Eight months before this celebrated conviction, in late January 1997, the highest-ranking *genocidaire* in Rwandan custody—and the first to be extradited from abroad—Froduald Karamira, was convicted of genocide and sentenced to death. He was an instigator, using vile and impassioned propaganda speeches to rally the masses of Hutus to kill. Throughout the trial he not only denied that the Tutsis had been exterminated, he denied that he had played any part in the killings—including the orders he gave to have his own neighbors killed. "I am accused of genocide," he said, "but what does that mean?"

It is in the International Tribunals that the difficulty of proving genocide and gaining a verdict has been made painfully clear. Between April and October of 1992, the organized destruction by the Serbian militia of a largely unarmed population of Bosnian Muslims was labeled a "war" and even a "civil war." Thanks to the UN embargo that locked into place a radical arms disparity between the Serbian army and the Bosnian army, militants shelled the defenders into submission. Then, without pause, they methodically and brutally butchered the unarmed men, women, and children.

Charged with crimes against humanity and genocide, the former Serbian leader, Slobodan Milosevic, died before the trial was completed, robbing those he targeted of even the satisfaction of a conviction for crimes against humanity. Many observers believe that during the lengthy trial prosecutors failed to provide the required evidence to get a genocide conviction, and thus, had Milosevic lived to be convicted, it probably would not have been for the crime of genocide. On September 27, 2006, a senior wartime leader of Bosnian Serbs, Momcilo Krajisnik, was sentenced to twenty-seven years in prison for "crimes against humanity" for his role in the campaign to turn large sections of Bosnia into an ethnically pure Serbian region, but he was acquitted on two counts of genocide. In her September 28, 2006, *New York Times* article, "Wartime Leader of Bosnian Serbs Receives 27-Year Sentence," Marlise Simons reported that Krajisnik's role, as spelled out by the prosecutors, was "to coordinate and oversee the brutal ethnic separation campaign carried out in thirty-seven Bosnian townships. Judges found him guilty of deportations, forced transfers and persecution as well as murder and extermination of Croats and Bosnian Muslims." The presiding judge, Alphonse Orie, read a summary of the judgment.

> The crimes were committed over a long period of time, often through brutal methods, with hatred or appalling lack of concern. The crimes constituted the actus reus of genocide, that is, when taken together they were acts of a genocidal nature.

What will it take to move from "*actus reus* of genocide" to a conviction of genocide? A lawyer following the procedures at the tribunal, Heikelina Verrijn Stuart, explained the difficulty to Marlise Simons:

> There is often a thin line between the crimes of deportation, persecution, extermination, which were

all admitted here, and the intention to commit genocide. In this case the judges drew the line, saying they did not get enough evidence that the genocidal intent existed.

Extermination admitted, but no proof of *intent* to commit genocide. As difficult as intent is to prove, Serbian and Muslim responses to the verdict and sentence demonstrate that even the trials are seen through two very different lenses—that of the perpetrators and that of those targeted. Serbs claimed that the courts held an anti-Serbian and a pro-Muslim bias, rather than a position of impartiality and neutrality. Muslims felt that the acquittal on genocide charges and the sentence of only twenty-seven years was an affront to the large number of Muslim civilians who were tortured, raped, and murdered.

> The ethical dimension of the word is such that using it designates the culprit and passes judgment on the executioner. In the absence of the moral dimension of the word, "genocide" becomes "massacre," or simply "self defense" or "legitimate defense."
> —JOSIAS SEMUJANGA, *ORIGINS OF THE RWANDAN GENOCIDE*

AN EMPTY SLOGAN, A BROKEN PROMISE

> If there is one thing sure in this world, it is certainly this: that it will not happen to us a second time.
> —PRIMO LEVI, *SURVIVAL IN AUSCHWITZ*

> It happened, therefore it can happen again: This is
> the core of what we have to say. It can happen, and it
> can happen everywhere.
> —PRIMO LEVI, *THE DROWNED AND THE SAVED*

It was at the end of World War II and in the aftermath of
the Nazi extermination of 6 million Jews and more than
5 million other human beings, including the near-total
annihilation of the Roma and Sinti—a cataclysmic event of
monumental horror—that the international community
swore "Never Again." "Never Again" is universally known
to stand for the world's line in the sand against such an
atrocity's recurrence. William Shawcross speaks truth to
power when he writes in the foreword to Alain Destexhe's
Rwanda and Genocide in the Twentieth Century that "Never
Again" "has been exposed as a slogan, not a promise."
James Waller, in his book *Becoming Evil, How Ordinary
People Commit Genocide and Mass Killing*, dubs the twentieth
century "The Age of Genocide." Noting that although "the
human reality of mass killings and genocide predated its
semantic taxonomy … the past century saw a massive scale
of systematic and intentional mass murder coupled with an
unprecedented efficiency of the mechanisms and techniques
of mass destruction." Despite the vow of "Never Again,"
genocides continue, unabated, while the world watches.

In his *Time* magazine column "How to Save Darfur,"
Peter Beinart quotes Freddy Umutanguha speaking in
Kigali, Rwanda: "If you don't protect the people of Darfur
today, never again will we believe you when you visit

Rwanda's mass graves, look us in the eye and say 'Never Again.'" Genocide is a reality for the people in the Sudan. And the risk of genocide remains frighteningly real for people in other hot spots in the world.

"Never Again" is a hollow slogan to the many who have survived the systematic dehumanization and attempt at extermination, only to see it happen again and again. Elie Wiesel, whose *Night* introduced me to the horrors of genocide, was more accurate when he wrote:

> Never shall I forget that night, the first night in the camp, that turned my life into one long night seven times sealed.
>
> Never shall I forget that smoke.
>
> Never shall I forget the small faces of children whose bodies I saw transformed into smoke under a silent sky.
>
> Never shall I forget those flames that consumed my faith forever.
>
> Never shall I forget the nocturnal silence that deprived me for all of eternity of the desire to live.
>
> Never shall I forget those moments that murdered my God and my soul and turned my dreams to ashes.
>
> Never shall I forget those things, even were I condemned to live as long as God himself.
>
> Never.

It is the survivors who never forget, who prick our conscience, who rail against the indifference of the international community, the indifference Roméo Dallaire wrote about in *Shake Hands with the Devil*. For "Never Again" to become more than a slogan, more than an empty promise, "we must eliminate from this earth the impunity with which the genocidaires were able to act, and re-emphasize the principle of justice for all, so that no one, for even a moment will make the ethical and moral mistake of ranking some humans as more human than others, a mistake that the international community endorsed by its indifference in 1994." We can no longer afford to be indifferent, as more survivors of more genocides never forget.

Will it happen again? It already has happened again, and again. But is it inevitable? That is a different question, begging for a completely different answer and explanation. Alain Destexhe, a former secretary general of Médecins Sans Frontières, writes about what happens when people explain that the killings of the Armenians, the Jews, and the Tutsis were due to background "circumstances": deeply entrenched inevitabilities of economic, tribal, cultural, religious differences; the death of a president; "excesses of crowds gripped by fear and ancient hatreds"; "man's inhumanity to man"; or the collateral damage of armed conflict:

> A consequence of this kind of reasoning is that "collective guilt" leaves us with no one to blame: no one admits to having chosen to become a Young Turk, a Nazi.... Therefore, so the argument continues, genocides and systematic massacres fall into the same category of disaster as volcanic eruptions or earth-

quakes. Carl Jung is quoted as saying, "The devil has always been around. He was there before the advent of human beings and he is the eternal principle that has corrupted them! So there will always be evil people.... Thus blaming the devil ... is a providential convenience." Where then lies guilt and responsibility if blame is laid on the devil, on "man's inhumanity to man," on circumstances or on destiny?—certainly it cannot then lie with any individual human beings.

It was individual human beings who premeditated, systematically planned, and executed these crimes of genocide. Wielding the power of the state, they *intended* to exterminate a group of human beings selected on the basis of their birth, religion, or culture. It is this *intentionality* to identify, target, and slaughter—as well as the murderous ideology of the state behind the intention—that is key to distinguishing genocide from all the other crimes against humanity.

Although the list I saw on the wall in Kigali numbered fourteen genocides, using the definition in the UN Genocide Convention one could argue convincingly that there were three definitive genocides in the twentieth century: that of the Armenians by the Young Turks, that of the Jews and Roma and Sinti by the Nazis, and that of the Tutsis by Hutu racists. And this is the definition—with its flaws and limitations—and these are the three genocides that I choose to use for my anatomy of genocide. In making these choices, I do not intend in any way to diminish or negate the other crimes against humanity, some of which may indeed be, and probably are, genocides. But, as Alain Destexhe explains, we must find other words to describe the tragedies that are not genocide, because

> [I]f not, the real meaning of genocide will continue to be trivialized and this most anti-human of all crimes will continue to be regarded as one more reason to justify fatalism. Genocide must be reinstated as the most infamous of crimes; the memory of the victims preserved and those responsible identified and brought to justice by the international community.

Separated out from the other crimes against humanity, the dissecting of this "most anti-human of all crimes" raises other questions. Does genocide occur along a continuum of violence, rather than as its own categorical course of action? There is a necessary distinction among the beating death of a young man who was gay (bullying gone lethal), lynching of black men in the American South (hate crimes), pogroms, and genocide, but is the distinction one of degree, not substance? Does this distinction matter, as Destexhe says it must? Does the use of weapons of mass destruction blur the lines and muddle the language of war and genocide? Does it matter that mass killings, where the boundaries of the targeted groups are less well defined than those of genocide, have psychological and cultural origins similar to genocide? Does the international community, individually and collectively, have a moral and legal obligation to intervene?

These questions, and the ensuing examination of genocide, bring into focus the very resolution set forth by the UN Convention and the contentious question of its amendment. What obligations are implied by a declaration of genocide? Do we wait for the declaration, or try to stop it before it begins? Is it possible to predict genocide? I think it is. Genocide does occur along a continuum, with clear, verifiable, and predictable signposts along the way leading to the final outcome of wholesale annihilation.

So what if we can forecast an imminent genocide, can actually see it coming? What guarantees do those who are targeted for extermination have that the world community will promptly and effectively intervene? In the words of genocide scholar Samuel Totten, formulating potential early-warning signals "is easy—and this is a vast understate-ment—compared to mobilizing the political will of the international community to act when such signals appear on the horizon." Countries that ratify the convention "undertake to prevent and to punish" genocide perpetrators and are entitled to call on the UN "to take such action under the Charter of the United Nations as they consider appropriate for the prevention and suppression of geno-cide." Is merely protesting and drawing up strongly worded resolutions and threats appropriate and enough?

The task before us is not merely to define genocide but to understand its nature, to "fathom its darkness," and thus perhaps to lift its veil of inevitability. The following chapter will deconstruct genocide, analyze genocide theory, and describe the conditions necessary for it to take place. In so doing, I will attempt to shatter some time-worn myths about this extraordinary evil and the humans who intentionally set out to exterminate an entire group of people.

> At the end of the day, no Geneva Convention on genocide, whatever its language, and no early warnings, however unmistakable, can substitute for political will among the powers-that-can. The extent of recent coverage of the Darfur tragedy suggests that media and public interest can indeed influence governments to appear to care. But garnering such interest, as Darfur plainly shows, is a long, drawn-out process, and the move from concern to action can take forever. Pessimists will not be disappointed.
>
> —GERALD CAPLAN, "THE GENOCIDE PROBLEM: 'NEVER AGAIN' ALL OVER AGAIN"

Chapter 2

Anatomy of Extraordinary Evil

History does not repeat itself; it rhymes.
—DAVID KAY, FORMER UNITED NATIONS
WEAPONS INSPECTOR

Just as *Romeo and Juliet* is to *West Side Story*, so too is the genocide of the Armenians in the Ottoman Empire to the genocide of the Jews, Roma, and Sinti in Nazified Europe, as are they both to the genocide of the Tutsis in Rwanda. Each has its own story line, setting, and characters but all have a common theme, common formula, and tragic outcome.

In studying all three genocides, I have found that each has its unique aspects, and yet there are startling parallels and connecting threads from any one to the others. The appeal of "Never Again" notwithstanding, each genocide appears to have set the stage for the next one. Hitler was emboldened by the impunity with which the Young Turks were able to pillage, rape, starve, and slaughter the Armenians. He is quoted as saying, "Who, after all, speaks today of the annihilation of the Armenians?" The Hutu extremists not only studied *Mein Kampf,* they modeled their "Hutu Ten Commandments" on Hitler's writings, speeches, and the infamous Nürnberg Laws.

One of the most chilling examples of the many threads that connect the genocides is contained in this paragraph, written by Robert Fisk in his tome *The Great War for Civilization: The Conquest of the Middle East.* Fisk credits Armenian historian Vahakn Dadrian with identifying Max Erwin von Scheubner-Richter as a key figure in the Nazi-led genocide of the Jews, Roma, and Sinti. Von Scheubner-Richter, a German vice-consul in the Armenian region of Erzerum, witnessed the massacres of Armenians in Bitlis province and reported to the German chancellor.

> In all, he submitted to Berlin fifteen reports on the deportations and mass killings, stating in his last message that with the exception of a few hundred thousand survivors, the Armenians of Turkey had been exterminated *(ausgerottet).* He described the methods by which the Turks concealed their plans for the genocide, the techniques used to entrap Armenians, the use of gangs, and even made a reference to the Armenians as "these 'Jews of the Orient' who are wily businessmen." Scheubner-Richter met Hitler only five years later and would become one of his closest advisors, running a series of racist editorials in the Munich newspaper which called for a "ruthless and relentless" campaign against Jews so that Germany should be "cleansed."

There are many other threads connecting these two genocides, and more Germans whose experiences in the Ottoman Empire during the genocide of the Armenians became useful to Hitler. Franz von Papen was chief of staff of the Fourth Turkish Army during the 1914–18 war and served as Hitler's vice-chancellor in 1933. During World War II, he was the Third Reich's ambassador to Turkey. Rudolf Hoess joined the German forces in Turkey as a teenager. In 1940 he was appointed commandant of Auschwitz, and he joined SS headquarters to become deputy-inspector of all Nazi concentration camps in 1944.

Practices were borrowed and improved upon. Stuffing Armenians into caves and setting a fire in the entrance to suffocate them en masse was a precursor to the gas chambers of the Nazis. Cramming Armenian men, women, and children into railway cattle cars for transport to their death in the Der Zor desert was witnessed in 1915 by Germans who worked for the Baghdad Railway Company. The German railway officials filed detailed reports to their superiors in Germany concerning the transports and the many rapes and murders and other atrocities that occurred along the tracks and in the camps set up near them.

When the perpetrators of the genocide in Darfur are called to account, will they bring with them a script that is eerily familiar, and will we find that the Rwandan genocide did indeed set the stage for Darfur's? And if the "sectarian violence" in Baghdad—or any other hot spot in the world—

proves to be not sectarian violence or civil war, but instead Act One of the tragedy known as genocide, will the world community turn a blind eye, as it did in Rwanda, give a passing nod to the term "genocide," and then fail to act, as we have done for far too long in Darfur? Will the perpetrators in Darfur be able to repeat the lines of the Ottoman Minister of the Interior, Mehmed Talaat? "It's no use for you to argue. We have already disposed of three quarters of the Armenians; there are none at all left in Bitlis, Van, and Erzerum. The hatred between the Turks and the Armenians is now so intense that we have got to finish with them."

I write this as fifty more tortured and mutilated bodies were found today floating down the Tigris in Iraq, just as tortured and mutilated bodies were found floating down the Tigris and the Euphrates rivers in 1915 and the Nyabarongo River in Rwanda in 1994.

> Each bloodletting hastens the next, and as the value of human life is degraded and violence becomes tolerated, the unimaginable becomes more conceivable.
>
> —PRESIDENT BILL CLINTON, DURING HIS BRIEF VISIT TO RWANDA, MARCH 25, 1998, AS HE EXPRESSED REGRET FOR HIS ACTS OF OMISSION AND ACTS OF COMMISSION THAT FACILITATED RATHER THAN HELPED TO STOP THE GENOCIDE OF THE TUTSIS

THE GENOCIDE OF THE ARMENIANS

All rights of the Armenians such as to live and work
on Turkish soil have been completely abrogated. In
reference to this, the government assumes all
responsibility and has ordered that even babes in
cradles are not to be spared.

> —MEHMED TALAAT, TURKISH MINISTER OF
> INTERNAL AFFAIRS, SEPTEMBER 9, 1915

The genocide of the Armenians took place during World
War I, between the years 1915 and 1918. It was planned,
administered, and executed by the ruling triumvirate of
Ismail Enver Pasha, Mehmed Talaat Pasha, and Jemal
Pasha, representing the party in power in the Turkish
government, the Committee of Union and Progress
(CUP), also known as the "Young Turks." Their target was
the entire Armenian population of the Ottoman Empire.

Before 1915 there were about 2 million Armenians in
Turkey; after the genocide there were fewer than one hundred
thousand. One out of three Armenians in the world was
killed. The Armenian people were subjected to deportation,
expropriation, abduction, torture, starvation, massacre, and
drowning. A large percentage of the Armenian population
was forcibly removed from Armenia and Anatolia to Syria.
Many were marched into the desert to die of thirst and
hunger. Others were methodically massacred throughout
the Empire; still others were taken out to sea and thrown
overboard to drown. Women and young girls were tortured
and raped; children were sold into slavery.

All property, belongings, and money—the entire wealth of the Armenian people—was confiscated by the government, or looted, extorted, and stolen along the deportation routes. Abram L. Sachar wrote of how the Turks even added a "note of macabre effrontery." Talaat asked American Ambassador Henry Morgenthau for "a list of Armenians who had been insured by American firms, for both the holders and the beneficiaries had been killed, and thus, by Turkish law, the Turkish Government was entitled to the residuary insurance estates!"

Between 1920 and 1923, the atrocities began anew. Any remaining Armenians were either expelled or massacred.

After World War I, many of the instigators and lead perpetrators of the genocide were tried—some in absentia, since they had fled the country—and found guilty of capital crimes. However, despite the moral outrage of the international community and the massive relief efforts mounted to "save the starving Armenians," no strong actions were taken to stop the genocide, or to hold the government itself responsible for its policies or for restitution to the surviving Armenians.

It is important to note that the three men who formed the triumvirate all fled and all met untimely deaths. Talaat was assassinated in Berlin in March 1921 by Soghomon Tehlirian, whose family had been killed in the genocide. Enver was killed in action against an Armenian battalion of the Red Army on August 4, 1922. Jemal was assassinated by Stepan Dzaghikian, Bedros Der Boghosian, and Ardashes Kevorkian in Tbilisi, Georgia.

THE GENOCIDE OF THE JEWS, ROMA, AND SINTI

No assessment of modern culture can ignore the fact that science and technology—the accepted flower and glory of modernity—climaxed in the factories of death.

—IRVING GREENBERG

Believing that the Germans were racially superior to the rest of the human race, and that the Jews were "life unworthy of life," the Nazis, who came to power in 1933, and their collaborators perpetrated the systematic, state-sponsored persecution, torture, and extermination of 6 million Jews and other "racially inferior" and "defective" human beings, including tens of thousands of Roma and Sinti. The Roma and Sinti were also made *"artfremd,"* "alien to the German species," at the 1935 Nazi Party convention in 1935 when the new racial laws were announced. In fact, the fate of the Roma and Sinti eerily paralleled that of the Jews, from labeling to deportation to extermination. Historians estimate that between 25 and 50 percent of all European Roma and Sinti were killed.

The implementation of the "Final Solution" began with the establishment of concentration camps to imprison Jews, Roma, and Sinti, along with other "undesirables," including people who were homosexual, and "political opponents" of the Nazis. The Nazis moved on to creating ghettos, transit camps, forced labor camps, mobile killing units, and extermination camps. By 1945, almost two out of every three European Jews had been killed.

The genocide ground to a halt as Allied forces liberated from the concentration and extermination camps the emaciated prisoners—many of whom had survived death marches, as well. World War II ended in Europe with the unconditional surrender of German armed forces in the west on May 7, 1945, and in the east on May 9, 1945.

It must be noted that although no Nazi was convicted of the crime of genocide of the Jews, at the Nürnberg trials no one was even accused, let alone tried, for the genocide of the Roma and Sinti. It would be almost fifty years later that Germany government officials would finally publicly acknowledge this genocide and be called to account for official recognition of the Nazis' crimes against the Roma and Sinti, for restitution similar to that sought by Jews, and for an end to legal discrimination. German Chancellor Helmut Kohl formally recognized the genocide in 1982. By then most of the Roma and Sinti eligible for restitution under German law were already dead.

THE GENOCIDE OF THE TUTSIS

We ... say to the *Inyenzi* [cockroaches] that if they lift up their heads again, it will no longer be necessary to go fight the enemy in the bush. We will ... start by eliminating the internal enemy.... They will disappear.
—HASSAN NGEZE, *KANGURA*, JANUARY 1994

On April 6, 1994, Rwandan President Juvénal Habyarimana's plane was shot down on its approach to the Kigali airport. Within the hour, the killings began. The death lists had been prepared in advance. Between April 6, 1994, and July 19, 1994, almost 1 million Tutsis and "moderate" Hutus—called "accomplices of Tutsis"—were killed in a series of well-planned, meticulously orchestrated attacks throughout Rwanda. The efficient system of local government, as well as the finely tuned chain of command from the central government in Kigali, allowed for the killing of at least 10,000 Tutsis each day, with many more humiliated, tortured, mutilated, and raped. Armed with primitive *masu* and machetes, guns, and grenades, the *genocidaires* killed at roadblocks, churches, schools, hospitals, and homes, in fields, marshes, and swamps. It was the most efficient genocide of the twentieth century.

THE RHYME AND REASON

Armenians cannot easily forget those earlier horrors
of this century, or accept denial of the realities of
history on the part of the Turkish government. For in
that continued denial there persists a threat to all
minorities.

—DR. V. L. PARSEGIAN, ARMENIAN PHYSICIST

It wasn't until the twentieth century that comparative studies of mass slaughter were seriously undertaken. Nor, until then, were the stories of the vanquished told. Up until the 1900s the mass killings of people of other races, nationalities, cultures, and religions were studied in the context of the conquerors and the winners, and as singular events in linear history.

The Battle of Little Big Horn and Custer's Last Stand happened at the same time, in the same place, with the same people, but the two story lines are worlds apart. And up until recently it was Custer's story line that most young people could repeat—unless those young people were descendants of the few First Nations survivors who, through word of mouth, handed down their own narrative, with all its pain and suffering and loss.

Even so, that event was seen as a part of one nation's history. Now such events are being studied through a clear lens of facts—facts that are fleshed out by the viewpoint of those targeted for mass extermination and those who were witnesses, resisters, and defenders, and they must be studied in relation to other, similar events in other countries and at other times. *First Nations History: We Were Not the Savages—Collision Between European and Native American Civilizations*, by Daniel N. Paul, is a prime example of such a project, as the author writes, "It must be discomforting to come to grips with the knowledge that one's ancestors were not always the kind gentle folks that some historians have depicted, but rather were barbaric in the way they treated other humans."

In *A Shameful Act: The Armenian Genocide and the Question of Turkish Responsibility*, historian and sociologist

Taner Akçam argues that the two mutually exclusive narratives and historiographical approaches to the period of the late 1800s and early 1900s in Turkish history "must be reconciled and viewed together: Their strong interrelationship is inextricably part of the same history." That is not to say that there are "two sides" to genocide, with each side merely a biased point of view. Professor Peter Balakian explains in *The Burning Tigris: The Armenian Genocide and America's Response* that any effort to present genocide as an event that has "two legitimate sides, and one that can be reduced to ethnic perspectives—the victims' and the perpetrators'—trivializes and defames a human rights crime of enormous magnitude." Akcam argues persuasively that the historiographical approach of the Turks to that period of time tells a story of "an empire dismembered by Europe's Great Powers, a drawn-out process of collapse and disintegration," a history of partition and demise—all true, but with a glaring omission, the genocide of the Armenians falling into the black hole of excuses and denial. Then there is the historiographical approach written by those targeted, which often excludes mention of the empire's partition, so insignificant a footnote in history in the minds of those who survived the attempt to wipe their people and culture off the face of the earth. Akcam goes on to explain that "for Turkey to become a truly democratic member of the society of nations, it has to confront this 'dark chapter,' this black hole of its history, this 'shameful act,' as Mustafa Kemal Ataturk, founder of the republic, called the Armenian genocide. Only full integration of Turkey's past can set the country on the path to democracy." And this history, as Richard G. Hovannisian notes, must be studied in relation to other events in other countries, at other times.

In his book *The Armenian Genocide: A Bibliography Relating to the Deportations, Massacres, and Dispersion of the Armenian People, 1915–1923*, Hovannisian lists the similarities of the genocide of the Armenians to the genocide of the Jews.

Had he added to his comparison the genocide of the Tutsis, he would have needed to make only one change: from "major international conflict" to "civil war" in number one. To add Darfur to the list, the change would have been that it is happening under the cover of a war between the government of Sudan (and its extralegal special armed forces) and *several* rebel groups. Perhaps what we are witnessing is one more leap from the genocides of the twentieth century to a more menacing form of genocide, or perhaps a more conscious awareness of human rights in the face of well-planned and well-executed exterminations—or both.

The similarities Hovannisian listed are (the material in parentheses is mine):

1. perpetration of the genocide under the cover of a major international conflict (the genocide of the Tutsis was under the cover of a civil war, Darfur under the cover of war against several rebel groups), thus minimizing the possibility of external intervention;
2. conception of the plan by a monolithic and megalomaniac coterie;

3. espousal of an ideology giving purpose and justification to chauvinism, racism, exclusivism, and intolerance toward the elements resisting assimilation;

4. imposition of strict party discipline and secrecy during the period of preparation;

5. formation of extralegal special armed forces to ensure the rigorous execution of the operation (Teshkilati Mattsusa by the Turks; SS and Einsatzgruppen by the Nazis; Interahamwe and "Network Zero" death squads by Hutu Power);

6. provocation of public hostility toward the targeted group and ascribing to it the very excesses to which it would be subjected;

7. certainty of the vulnerability of the intended prey;

8. exploitation of advances in mechanization and communication to achieve unprecedented means for control, coordination, and thoroughness;

9. use of sanctions such as promotions and the incentive to loot, plunder, and vent passions without restraint; or

10. conversely the dismissal and punishment of reluctant officials;

11. the intimidation of persons who might consider harboring members of the targeted group.

If all of these genocides use this same outline for their script, conversely, the appearance of any one of these actions could serve as an early warning of the potential for an impending genocide. By understanding the nature of the beast, perhaps it is possible not to just compare genocides after they have occurred but to more clearly recognize warning signs and develop concrete plans to put them in check. Perhaps it is possible to see it coming, stop it in its tracks, and, most important of all, prevent it.

> [T]he Armenian massacre was the greatest crime of the war, and the failure to act against Turkey is to condone it ... the failure to deal radically with the Turkish horror means that all talk of guaranteeing the future peace of the world is mischievous nonsense.
> —PRESIDENT THEODORE ROOSEVELT IN A MAY 11, 1918, LETTER TO CLEVELAND H. DODGE

THE GORILLA IN OUR MIDST: WAR AND GENOCIDE

As Lemkin noted, war and genocide are almost always connected. The Ottomans killed more than 1 million Armenians during World War I, and the Germans exterminated 6 million Jews and 5 million Poles, Roma, homosexuals, political opponents, and others during World War II. Iraq later targeted its Kurdish minority during the Iran-Iraq war; Bosnian Serbs set out to destroy Muslims and Croats during a Balkan civil war; and Rwandan Hutu nationalists exterminated some 800,000 Tutsi while the Rwandan army also fought a more conventional civil war against a Tutsi rebel force.... For outsiders, war between armies can also mask genocide, making it initially difficult to discern eliminationist campaigns

against civilians and inviting customary diplomatic
efforts.

—SAMANTHA POWER, *A PROBLEM FROM HELL:*
AMERICA AND THE AGE OF GENOCIDE

Another critical requirement for stopping genocide in its
tracks is to see it for what it really is. Though the term
genocide has been defined and encoded in law since the
mid-twentieth century, the atrocities of the crime are still
most often named as such only after the fact. It is, of
course, in the interests of any genocidal regime to create a
context that distracts attention from the true nature of its
goals and behaviors, and the rhetoric of war and conflict
lends itself to this effort.

We, as observers, can have a disinclination to see and
acknowledge for what it is the extraordinary evil that is
genocide, to accept that our fellow humans might be
capable of this kind of atrocity. And our unwillingness to
see is abetted by a common phenomenon of observation.

In a 1999 research project conducted by Daniel Simons
and Christopher Chabris, subjects were asked to view a
seventy-five-second video titled *Gorilla in Our Midst:*
Sustained Inattentional Blindness for Dynamic Events. On
the video, two teams—one dressed in white, one dressed
in black—passed two basketballs around. The subjects
were to count the number of passes between players
wearing the same color. About forty-five seconds into the
video a woman wearing a gorilla suit walks through the
group of players, stops briefly to pound her chest, and
then continues walking out of the video frame—spending

a total of nine seconds on the screen. Subjects who were counting the passes were then asked if they had seen the gorilla. Only 36 percent reported that they had. The other 64 percent experienced what is known as "inattentional blindness," the inability to detect unexpected objects to which we aren't paying attention.

As Samantha Power notes, acts of war, and even just the rhetoric of war, can have the effect of masking genocide. In this sense, the "eliminationist campaigns" are the unexpected objects, the "gorilla in our midst" to which "outsiders" aren't paying attention.

Those who instigate and perpetrate the eliminationist campaigns actually use war as a *tool* of genocide. Wartime conditions heighten the threat level and create a polarized world view in which the "enemy" is objectified and dehumanized; those targeted for extermination are thus easily subsumed into the category of enemy and measures are allowed that would not be tolerated in peacetime. As well, the perpetrators are provided with the necessary cover to carry out their ugly deeds. Genocide is not the *cause* or *consequence* of war.

In his memoirs, Mehmed Talaat Pasha wrote: "Any abuses were fairly typical if 'regrettable' features of war, carried out by 'uncontrolled elements.'" In June 1915, Talaat laid bare the lie originally told by the government that the Armenians "were being moved out of harm's way for their own good and protection during the war." He shared with Dr. Mordtmann of the German Embassy his true intent behind the deportation and subsequent extermination of the Armenians: "The Sublime Porte [government of the Ottoman Empire] intends to make use of the world war in order to thoroughly liquidate *(grundlich aufzaumen)* its internal enemies, the local Christians, so that foreign countries won't hinder doing it by diplomatic interference. This measure will serve to the interests of all allies of Turkey, especially the Germans, and so the latters will be able to consolidate...." Dr. Martin Niepage, a teacher in the German Technical School at Aleppo, wrote a note to the German Accredited Representative and said:

> I was told that, in various quarters of Allepo, there were lying masses of half-starved people, the survivors of so-called "deportation convoys." In order, I was told, to cover the extermination of the Armenian nation with a political cloak, military reasons were being put forward, which were said to make it necessary to drive the Armenians out of their native seats, which had been theirs for 2,500 years, and to deport them to the Arabian deserts.

On August 22, 1939, in a meeting in Obersalzburg, Adolf Hitler told his military chiefs, "The aim of war is not to reach definite lines but to annihilate the enemy physically. It is by this means that we shall obtain the vital living space that we need. Who today still speaks of the massacre of the Armenians?" The Nazi regime assimilated the language of genocide into the more conventional and comfortable narrative of war: all Jews were at war with

Nazi Germany. There was an international conspiracy perpetrated by the Jews and their puppet governments of Britain, the Soviet Union, and the United States to annihilate Germans. Bolshevism was the Jews' declaration of war against culture. The Nazis saw Nazism as a national struggle for freedom against the chains of slavery imposed by Jews.

In his diary entry for March 27, 1942, Dr. Joseph Goebbels wrote:

> A punishment is being meted out to the Jews that is indeed barbaric but they however completely deserve ... one cannot allow sentimentality in these matters. If we hadn't defended ourselves against them, the Jews would exterminate us. It is a battle of life and death between the Aryan race and the Jewish bacillus.... Here as in other matters, the Führer is the steadfast champion and spokesman of a radical solution, which this situation demands and which therefore appears to be unavoidable. Thank God that now, during wartime, we have a whole series of opportunities that would be closed off to us in peace time. Hence, we need to use them ... Jewry has nothing to laugh about ...

In the article "Who Will Survive the War of March?" published in the government-supported paper *Kangura*, the writer accuses the Rwandan Patriotic Front (RPF) of planning to take power by force, and the United Nations

Assistance Mission to Rwanda (UNAMIR) of taking sides with the RPF against the Hutu government. One of the ploys of Hutu extremists was to allege that the RPF was going to inflict genocide on the Hutus, that the Tutsis had prepared graves for the Hutus, and that the Tutsis, through family-planning clinics, were manipulating the birth rates of the Hutus. Stanislas Mbonampeka, former Minister of Justice, who went over to the "dark side," to the side of Hutu Power, explained to Philip Gourevitch that he believed that in war one cannot be neutral: "Personally I don't believe in the genocide. This was not a conventional war. The enemies were everywhere. The Tutsis were not killed as Tutsis, only as sympathizers of the RPF."

For the *genocidaires*, "inviting customary diplomatic efforts" is not a mistake but a calculated, diabolical plan to ensure that the genocide can proceed unhampered by intrusive measures that would be required of outsiders to stop the slaughter if it were seen as genocide, not a civil war. Knowing full well that the signing of the Arusha Accords would give the pretense of warring parties nego-tiating for peace, thus "inviting customary diplomatic efforts," the Hutu extremists in the government went along with the charade and at the same time ramped up their plans for the extermination of the Tutsis.

Assigned to "keep the peace" in Rwanda after the signing of the Arusha Accords, UN Force Commander for UNAMIR Roméo Dallaire was expected to follow the principles of *neutrality*, *impartiality*, and *explicit consent* of the parties, as these were the orienting concepts and rules that governed any UN peacekeeping mission. But in November and December of 1983 there were several large-scale attacks on civilians. On December 3, military officers spoke of a "diabolical" plot to make a mockery of the Arusha Accords, and an informant warned of the impending genocide. In his January 11, 1994, communiqué to the UN, Roméo Dallaire warned of the stockpiling of arms, a detailed "hit list," and explicit extermination plans. He asked for permission to seize the arms caches. The response he received was that UNAMIR was to abide by the rules of *neutrality, impartiality,* and *explicit consent.* The memo ended with

> If you have major problems with the guidance provided above, you may consult us further. We wish to stress, however, that the overriding consideration is the need to avoid entering into a course of action that might lead to the use of force and unanticipated consequences.

The January 11 cable was a warning that should have been impossible to miss, and the targeted killings in April should have solidified the nature of this crime as genocide. The problem was that in the minds of the United Nations and the world community this was being scripted as "ancient tribal animosities," "chaotic fighting between warring factions," a civil war with "unfortunate civilian killings." In *Eyewitness to a Genocide*, Michael Barnett offers a disturbing account of why the United Nations failed to act while almost 1 million human beings were hacked to death in Rwanda:

> There was the plain fact that the RPF and the government had resumed war. But the tendency to treat all violence as related to civil war derived from a prior understanding of the nature of the Rwandan conflict and the assumption that this presumed past could be mapped directly onto current circumstances.... The accepted script was that UNAMIR was to oversee a cease-fire and resolve a civil war between two contending ethnic groups.... When the violence did return, all eyes in New York assumed they were seeing a civil war....
>
> [Boutros-Ghali and his staff] consistently portrayed the violence as "chaotic" and spontaneous, projecting an image of killing that was reciprocal and multi-sided.... The Secretariat adopted a vocabulary that body checked the intervention camp.

Roméo Dallaire had no peace to keep; the gorilla was not just pounding its chest, it was leaving in its wake a trail of blood; and the world stood by, stricken with inattentional blindness. The resumption of the civil war became the cover and pretext for the genocide. Once it was framed as a civil war, the range of responses was restricted to consent-based alternatives for resolving a conflict. There can be no consent, no neutrality, no impartiality when one group is hell-bent on exterminating the other.

During my July 2006 meeting with President Paul Kagame, we discussed the "inattentional blindness" that even Roméo Dallaire exhibited on the third day of the genocide, still seeking to use conflict resolution and peacekeeping strategies to end the "conflict." Dallaire asked Kagame, as the head of the RPF, to come to Kigali to meet with the deputy commander of the Rwandan Armed Forces (FAR), General Gatsinzi (who was not a part of the extremists' plot), Colonel Théoneste Bagosora, and other leaders (all involved either in orchestrating and/or carrying out the genocide, but supposedly willing to talk about some sort of peace agreement with the RPF). When Kagame asked how he was supposed to travel safely from the RPF camp to the capital, Dallaire offered to send a UN helicopter. Kagame laughed and said the *genocidaires* would shoot it down. Dallaire then offered to come with two helicopters, one to bring him to Kigali and the other as an escort, for protection. Smiling, Kagame told me that his response to Dallaire was: "Some won't care if it is a UN helicopter. They'll just shoot both of us down."

Paul Kagame saw the "gorilla in our midst." He knew that he had to achieve a military victory *and* end the genocide simultaneously. A few hours after the offer of the helicopter, he called Dallaire again and told him that either the UN had to act immediately to stop the massacres, or the RPF would intervene "to rescue our people ... we are coming, just take note."

In his book *Paul Kagame and Rwanda*, Colin M. Waugh writes about how quickly the RPF swept across the countryside. As it did, "its troops began to discover massacre sites and encountered victims fleeing with machete wounds to their heads and bodies, the first evidence for many in the invading force of the trauma which had been unfolding behind government lines. Large numbers of Tutsis took refuge in areas cleared by the RPF as safe havens while the main force moved onwards."

Within days, Dallaire, too, saw "the gorilla in our midst." In his twice-daily reports to UN headquarters, he described the violence not as a conflict, but as "ethnic cleansing in its most sinister form" and pleaded for reinforcements to demonstrate a show of international force to stand down the *genocidaires* and to protect civilians. When told that the UN mission might be abandoned, Dallaire refused, on moral grounds, to leave his post, and with his rapidly dwindling and ill-equipped troops he continued to rescue whomever he could and give witness to the rest of the world of what was happening. In his memoirs, Dallaire wrote that on April 24 the non-governmental relief organization Oxfam was the first organization to call the violence what it was—not ethnic cleansing, not even ethnic cleansing in its most sinister form, but genocide. From there on, Dallaire used the term "genocide" in all his correspondence and media reports.

Meanwhile, the UN "remained actively seized of the matter"; in other words, debate continued. There was too much attention to the fighting and too little attention to the killing. Since the UN peacekeeping mandate was to anticipate and prevent the return of "civil war," the

Council refused even to acknowledge the fact that, with UN assistance, it was the RPF that could even more quickly stop the genocide. But once again, inattentional blindness set in as the Council threatened to pull UNAMIR out completely and refused to lend support to "one of the two combatants," because doing so would mean violating its policies and rules of *neutrality, impartiality,* and *explicit consent.* In a *Toronto Star* news report on April 21, 1994—"UN Troops Pray as They Scramble Out of Rwanda"—Special UN Representative to Rwanda Jacques Booh-Booh is quoted as saying that if the "warring parties do not reach an agreement on a cease-fire, it must be very clear we shall not stay here. We came to assist Rwanda but we cannot impose any solution on the Rwandan people, who have to help us help them."

In May 1994, as the genocide was in full swing, the United States issued a presidential directive that restricted future peacekeeping involvement of any United States troops, inadvertently guaranteeing through these directives that *genocidaires* could carry out their extermination plans without fear of American troop intervention. With veto power in the UN Security Council, the United States was at the same time all but guaranteeing the impediment to the deployment of any UN troops to intervene to prevent or stop a massacre. The criteria for involvement included

1. The pre-existence of a ceasefire.
2. A commitment to a peace process between the parties in conflict.

3. Co-involvement of regional or subregional organizations.
4. The formulation of a precise mandate.
5. The existence of a clear political goal.
6. The reasonable assurance of the safety of UN personnel.

All of these criteria make sense if dealing with warring parties willing to come to the peace table; none of these make any sense in the face of genocide.

And it was not only myopic vision that was used as an excuse to keep from calling the extermination of Tutsis "genocide. " The expression "acts of genocide," as a separate activity from "real genocide," was used for the sake of convenience, and as an escape from the moral imperative that would be created by calling the extermination of the Tutsis genocide. In a press conference on June 10, 1994, U.S. State Department spokesperson Christine Shelly was challenged by a correspondent for Reuters News Service, Alan Elsner, to describe the events taking place in Rwanda. Following the guidance given by Secretary of State Warren Christopher that officials were authorized to state only that "acts of genocide" had occurred in Rwanda, Shelly responded, "Based on the evidence we have seen from observations on the ground, we have every reason to believe acts of genocide have occurred in Rwanda." Elsner then asked the difference between "acts of genocide" and "genocide." Following the party line, Shelly responded, "Well, I think the—as you know, there's a legal definition of this.... Clearly not all of the killings that have taken place in Rwanda are killings to which you might apply that label ... but as to the distinction between the words, we're trying to call what we have seen so far as best we can; based, again, on the evidence, we have every reason to believe that acts of genocide have occurred." Elsner then asked the potent question, "How many acts of genocide does it take to make a genocide?" Shelly's comment was no real response: "Alan, that's just not a question that I am in a position to answer."

On that very same day, in his story for the *New York Times*, "Official Told to Avoid Calling Rwanda Killings 'Genocide,'" Douglas Jehl quoted David Rawson, U.S. ambassador to Rwanda: "As a responsible government, you don't just go round hollering 'genocide.' You say that acts of genocide may have occurred and they need to be investigated." By June 10, 1994, the streets, the schools, the churches, and the River Nyaborongo were littered with more than 800,000 dead men, women, and children, and this crime that once had no name was to remain nameless, lest a signatory to the treaty be morally—and legally—obligated to act.

Inattentional blindness was now paired with ruthless self-interest, a policy of non-involvement, and a lack of imagination to fathom, even in the face of graphic media coverage, the extraordinary evil being perpetrated by a genocidal government. In *A Problem from Hell: America and the Age of Genocide*, Samantha Power describes the distorted thinking behind such a presidential directive as a desire on the part of American policymakers, journalists, and civilians to believe that the actors in this scenario will behave rationally and will not inflict gratuitous violence: "They trust in good-faith negotiations and traditional diplomacy. Once the killings start, they assume that civilians who keep their heads down will be left alone. They urge ceasefires and donate humanitarian aid."

Alain Destexhe, seeing clearly what was happening on the ground in Rwanda, knew the consequences of "non-involvement," the folly of good-faith negotiations, and the futility of traditional diplomacy in dealings with a genocidal state government.

> There were two things the UN could have done, neither of which it did: it could have made a selective intervention to protect the hospitals, schools and other places where the Tutsi were desperately seeking refuge and it could have clearly recognized the RPF as the legitimate government of Rwanda and so broken off relations with the government that had initiated the genocide. Such measures could have changed the course of Rwandan history.

The moral imperative for intervention trumped the peacekeeping mandate—a mandate that was totally inappropriate and counterproductive in the face of such a beast. The killing of a woman by the Interahamwe militiamen in front of the United Nations peacekeeping troops was shown on live TV. When asked by a journalist why the peacekeeping troops did not intervene, they replied that they did not have a mandate to do so. In fact, rather than drop the peacekeeping mandate in the midst of genocide, the UN Security Council was willing to shut down UNAMIR and pull the remaining peacekeepers out of Rwanda.

In an attempt to protect foreign policy interests in the region—and probably to look good on the home front—on June 15, France offered to provide humanitarian assistance to Rwanda. Skeptical of France's motives, the Security Council insisted, "The strictly humanitarian character of this operation ... shall be conducted in an impartial and neutral fashion, and shall not constitute an interposition force between the parties." On June 22, the Security Council gave the go ahead for "Operation Turquoise." This time the "gorilla in our midst" was provided safe passage out of the scene when, on July 9, France established a "safe humanitarian zone" in southwestern Rwanda. (To its credit, the operation did save several thousand Tutsis in the security zone.) As the RPF advanced, almost 1.2 million people fled toward Zaire. The displaced included Rwandan troops and many known *genocidaires*. Under the guise of the humanitarian character of its operation, France ensured that no French soldiers would arrest any known *genocidaires*, or seek out and destroy the transmitters for the *genocidaires'* Radio Mille Collines, which continued to spew its hate-filled broadcasts from the Operation Turquoise zone. As the known leaders of the genocide were fleeing to the humanitarian zone and on to the refugee camps, Roméo Dallaire requested permission from UN headquarters to go after and arrest them. Once again he was denied, because his superiors at the UN saw this as a violation of the peacekeeping mandate.

TRYING TO STOP a genocide by using tools that are effective in stopping armed conflicts is futile, naive, and dangerous. This blame-on-all-sides position—that genocide is a two-sided affair; that both sides were willing and equal parties; that both got what they had coming to them; that both were equally responsible for the "fray"; that the target invited the attack and thus deserved it—not only falsifies the difference between the methodical genocide and armed conflict but also leads to political equalizing and reinforces another myth espoused for causes of genocide, the theory of "ancient animosities": "These tribes have been fighting for generations."

The "gorilla in our midst" is not party to any form of conflict resolution—be it negotiation, truce, disarmament, or reason. Both genocide's inception and its solution lie elsewhere. Armed conflict can and indeed has been *resolved* through some form of conflict resolution—often with third-party participation or intervention. Genocide must be *stopped* by a third party, perpetrators brought to justice, reparation made, and the community healed through restorative justice. And if healing is not yet possible, people must be able to coexist in community, all of which I will address further in the last chapter.

Viewing genocide as a dispute to be resolved, a rift to be healed, or even as an armed conflict is to dishonor those who were gassed, hacked with machetes, burned, and butchered by ordinary people systematically and methodically committing acts of extraordinary evil.

By viewing the genocide as a conflict and adamantly hanging onto the mantra of *neutrality, impartiality, and consent,* the world community failed Rwandan Tutsis. The RPF succeeded on its own in ending the genocide on July 19, 1994.

> The [UN Security] council saw the situation in
> Rwanda as a "civil war," "ethnic conflict," and a
> "failed state" all rolled into one, terms that seemed
> as naturally connected as "peacekeeping" and
> "consent." ... In retrospect it is known that Rwanda
> was not a failed state. To carry out this level of
> killing in such a short time requires a tight chain of
> command, discipline, and an organization that is
> hardly reflective of a failed state. But the discursive
> inferno of civil war consumed the oxygen for other
> possibilities.
> —MICHAEL BARNETT, *EYEWITNESS TO A GENOCIDE*

Chapter 3

Genocide: Bullying to the Extreme

Hate has a nearly limitless ability to dehumanize
its victims, shutting down the most basic human
capacities for sympathy and compassion.

—RUSH W. DOZIER, JR., *WHY WE HATE:
UNDERSTANDING, CURBING, AND ELIMINATING
HATE IN OURSELVES AND OUR WORLD*

As I mentioned in the introduction, it was a lecture I
gave at the University of Rwanda in Butare that reframed
my 2005 trip to Africa—and subsequently resulted in the
writing of this book. In Butare, using the Rwandan genocide as a particular case in point, I demonstrated that
genocide is in fact the most extreme form of the drama
known as bullying, perpetrated by ordinary human beings
who go home to dinner after deeply humiliating and then
killing men, women, and children. By conceding that
genocide is not outside the realm of ordinary human
behavior, we can then begin to examine its roots and the
climate that facilitates its pathological growth.

It is important to remember that bullying does not

include criminal activity that might have begun as a conflict before escalating to conflict with weapons. Such activity falls under the category of armed conflict and, when ramped up, war. In these circumstances, any and all of the tools in the toolbox for conflict resolution, mediation, and peacekeeping can be helpful if used skillfully, and if both parties are willing to seek a productive solution. However, some violent activities do bear the markers of bullying as well as of criminality. These are commonly called "hate crimes": criminal acts against a person, group of people, or property in which the bully chooses the target because of the target's real or perceived race, religion, gender, sexual orientation, national origin, disability, or ethnicity, and which, when legitimized, institutionalized, and politicized, can progress to genocide. These distinctions are critical to the argument I am making that

sibling conflict is to armed conflict is to war

as

bullying is to criminal bullying (hate crime) is to genocide

and

war can be a tool of genocide.

Starting with this premise, one can see the path leading from the first scenes of schoolyard bullying to this act of extraordinary evil—this Final Solution. In a genocide, a bully (often a "bullied bully") rises to power, is elected to political office, or seizes control of a government. The bully then espouses a murderous racial, ethnic, or religious ideology, brings along an entire cast of characters, and goes about creating increasingly sinister scenes of what psychiatrist Robert Lifton calls "atrocity producing situations." As Lifton describes it, "in environments where sanctioned brutality becomes the norm, sadistic impulses, dormant in all of us, are likely to be expressed. The group's violent energy becomes such that an individual ... who questions it could be turned upon." These situations, in turn, invite and sustain ordinary citizens as they participate in the "extermination" of relatives, neighbors, and fellow citizens. The more that ordinary people perform such tasks as hacking someone to death, the more they become socialized to the atrocity, the more the atrocity becomes normalized—made ordinary. Thus it becomes "all in a day's work" to take out to sea a few hundred people and throw them overboard to drown; shove a few thousand people into the gas chambers and them shovel them into the crematorium; hack to death with *masu* and machetes a few more thousand Tutsis.

BULLYING—WHAT IT IS AND WHAT IT ISN'T

Mass killing or genocide is usually the outcome of an evolution that starts with discrimination and limited acts of harm doing. Harming people changes the perpetrators (and the whole society) and prepares them for more harmful acts.

ERVIN STAUB, "THE PSYCHOLOGY OF BYSTANDERS, PERPETRATORS, AND HEROIC HELPERS"

In discussing the continuum on which both bullying and genocide can be situated, it is important first to clearly make the distinction between ordinary conflict, which is normal, natural, and necessary, and bullying, which isn't. I explained to the students in Butare that as I researched anti-bullying programs throughout the world for my book *The Bully, the Bullied, and the Bystander,* what alarmed me was that many had as their foundation conflict-resolution solutions. The problem here is that bullying is not about anger or conflict; it is about contempt—a powerful feeling of dislike toward somebody considered to be worthless, inferior, or undeserving of respect. Children who work through these anti-bullying programs are skilled in handling all different kinds of conflict and learn anger management skills, but they still have no clue as to how to identify and effectively confront bullying.

Even more alarming, it was this same frame of reference that the international community used to devise procedures to intervene in the genocide of the Tutsis, and that it continues to use to devise procedures to deal with the genocide in Darfur. The mistake here is in seeing both as conflicts, while "the discursive inferno of civil war consumed the oxygen for other possibilities." And the gorilla continues to roam the landscape undetected and undeterred.

Conflicts are disagreements or clashes between people, ideas, or principles. They are a normal, natural, and necessary part of our lives. Children will fight. Our job as wise and caring adults is to teach them to work through their conflicts directly, creatively, nonviolently—not passively or aggressively—and to help them reach fair, equitable, and just solutions and resolutions. No easy task, to be sure.

A more difficult task is for nation states to handle their conflicts in such a fashion. Nevertheless, the world community has devised tools to help warring states negotiate a peace. A third party is introduced—be it a mediator or peacekeeping force—and is expected to operate with the explicit consent of both parties, acting in a neutral and impartial fashion. These are the same expectations children have of an intervening third party, but for warring states the situation is more dire, the stakes are higher, and the potential consequences are often irretrievable and irreversible.

None of these tools—including the language of conflict—is helpful in the case of genocide. Conflict, when not resolved nonviolently, can escalate to armed conflict and to all-out war. Conflict does *not* escalate to genocide. Bullying can.

To begin to fathom genocide, the place to start is not with conflict but with bullying. Bullying is a conscious, willful, deliberate activity intended to harm, to induce fear through the threat of further aggression, and to create terror in the target. Whether it is premeditated or seems to come out of the blue, is obvious or subtle, "in your face" or behind your back, easy to identify or cloaked in the garb of apparent friendship, done by one person or by a group, bullying always includes these three elements:

1. Imbalance of power: The bully can be older, stronger, higher up the social ladder, a different race or religion,

or of the opposite sex. Sheer numbers of people banded together can create the imbalance.

2. Intent to harm: The bully means to inflict emotional and/or physical pain, expects the action to hurt, and often takes pleasure in witnessing the hurt.

3. Threat of further aggression: Both the bully and the bullied know the bullying can and probably will occur again. This is not meant to be a one-time event.

When bullying escalates unabated, a fourth element is added:

4. Terror: Bullying is systematic violence used to intimidate and maintain dominance. Terror struck in the heart of the person targeted is not only a means to an end; it is an end in itself.

Once terror is created, the bully can act without fear of recrimination or retaliation. The bullied person is rendered so powerless that he or she is unlikely to fight back. The bully counts on bystanders becoming involved in participating or supporting the bullying or at least doing nothing to stop it. Thus the cycle of violence begins.

Bullying is a learned behavior. People have to learn to treat another person with contempt, to see that person as less than them, not worthy of their respect, and outside of their "circle of caring." For the 1949 Broadway musical *South Pacific*, Oscar Hammerstein II wrote these lyrics for the song "You've Got to Be Carefully Taught."

You've got to be taught
To hate and fear,
You've got to be taught
From year to year,
It's got to be drummed
In your dear little ear
You've got to be carefully taught.

You've got to be taught to be afraid
Of people whose eyes are oddly made,
And people whose skin is a diff'rent shade,
You've got to be carefully taught.

You've got to be taught before it's too late,
Before you are six or seven or eight,
To hate all the people your relatives hate,
You've got to be carefully taught!

The song's straightforward message is that hatred is not innate but rather learned. More often than not, young children are not instructed *explicitly* to consider others "inferior" or "unworthy"; these concepts are not so much *taught* as *caught*. The biases at the foundation of this contempt are often deeply rooted attitudes found in our homes, our schools, our religions, and our society. Any bias or prejudice related to race, gender (including sexual orientation), religion, physical attributes, mental abilities, or social and economic standing can and will be used by a bully to validate and justify contempt for an individual or a whole group.

Just as bullying can range from mild to moderate to severe, so can contempt range from disregard to scorn to cold hate—the devaluation of another human being to the point of placing him or her outside the web of moral obligation.

Bigotry can be caught in hearing nursery rhymes that negatively stereotype a group of people, singing songs that denigrate individuals, groups, or an entire culture, chanting rants that urge violence against a group, and repeating clichés that reinforce negative stereotypes. ("I 'jewed' him down." "She 'gypped' me.") Intolerance can be learned along with addition and subtraction. On a recent trip to Rwanda, a young woman showed me a worksheet she had completed when she was a child in primary school in the 1960s. One of the math problems read, "If you have ten cockroaches in your town and you kill four of them, how many do you have left to kill?" One of the cruel euphemisms for Tutsis that all elementary schoolchildren in Rwanda knew was "cockroach." In his latest book, *Five Germanys I Have Known*, Fritz Stern tells how in 1933 his math teacher, Herr Müth, gave the class word problems such as: "If three Jews robbed a bank, and each got a part of the loot proportionate to their ages ... how much would each get?"

Contempt can be fueled through billboard messages. In the mid-1930s, anti-Semitic slogans began showing up on roadside signs in Germany: "Trust not the fox on green heath, and not the Jew when he gives his oath." It is a testament to the power of such a "catchy bit of cultural poison" that Fritz Stern could recall that sign seventy years later. Poems and songs were also used in all three genocides to reinforce stereotypes and prejudices that in turn laid the groundwork for discrimination.

Contempt can also be buried in dispassionate language. In a telegram sent to the acting commander of Turkey's Fifth Army Corps, a recruitment bureau chief wrote, "The Armenian vermin gathered tonight from the townships and villages have been led to the predetermined places." It was in these predetermined places that men, women, and children were then humiliated, tortured, raped, and killed—eliminated with the cold contempt with which one would rid a house of rats or cockroaches.

The Nazis were masterful in creating media messages— using radio, street posters, animated movies, slogans, and rituals—that clearly separated the "pure Aryan race" from the "vermin" that ate at the fabric of the *Volk.*" In Rwanda the extremists utilized all forms of media to spew racist ideology, creating fear that the Tutsis were planning to kill all the Hutus and rallying the people to "chop down the trees, bring in the cabbage, kill the cockroaches, do your work to clear the community of filth." The radio—the main means of communication throughout the country—was also used to announce the whereabouts of targeted individuals, their addresses, car license plate numbers, and the numbers and names of family members who needed to be killed.

Once human beings feel the cold hate of contempt for other human beings, they can do anything to them and feel no compassion, guilt, or shame; in fact, they often get pleasure from the targeted person's pain. This contempt comes packaged with three *apparent* psychological advantages:

1. A sense of entitlement—the supposed privilege and right to control, dominate, subjugate, and otherwise abuse another human being. (The Young Turks held a belief in *Millet-I Hakime* [ruling nation], i.e., Muslim Turks were superior to all other peoples and had the inherent right to rule. Hitler felt that Providence had chosen him as savior of the German nation. Under Rwanda's President Habyarimana, Hutu extremists cultivated a political ideology that was racist and fascist, mixing feelings of deep grievance and belief in absolute power with privilege and patronage.)

2. An intolerance toward differences—*different* equals *inferior* and thus *not worthy of respect*. (The leaders of the genocides presented to their followers a Manichaean message that pitted the pure against the impure; the human against the subhuman; Turk, Aryan, Hutu versus *"gavur"* [infidel], *"rayah"* [cattle], bacteria, and vermin; Bantu versus Hamites.)

3. A liberty to exclude—to bar, isolate, and segregate a person deemed not worthy of respect or care. ("Witch hunts" against "infidels" were implemented as government policy; laws were enacted that marginalized, segregated, restricted, ostracized, and excluded the targeted groups.)

These are only *apparent* advantages because they are built on the false assumption that some humans are more human than others. In this way, bullying is arrogance in action. People who bully have an air of superiority that is often—though not always—a mask to cover up deep hurt and feelings of inadequacy. Bullies rationalize that their supposed superiority entitles them to harm unmercifully someone they hold in contempt, when in reality they are often putting someone down so they can feel "up." Some of the most prominent Hutu extremists were Tutsis whose families changed their ethnic identity cards. Others were the children of Tutsi mothers, and thus in a vulnerable and inferior position in a Hutu-dominated society. Armenian historian Ara Baliozian has defined this inferiority complex as "arrogance that has been mortally wounded."

Dr. Joseph Goebbels, one of the main mouthpieces for Nazi propaganda, displayed this arrogance as he delivered his last speech, on the evening of April 19, 1945:

> [I]nternational Jewry froths at the mouth as the driver behind the scenes. It does not want peace until it has realized its satanic goal of the destruction of the world. It seeks this goal in vain. As he has so often in the past when he stood before the door of power over all peoples, God will again push Lucifer back into the abyss from which he came.

The "God" that Goebbels was talking about was his boss, Adolf Hitler. Twelve days after this speech, on May 1, 1945, it was Joseph Goebbels who was frothing at the mouth, his arrogance mortally wounded. After his wife poisoned all six of their children, she and Goebbels committed suicide by taking cyanide pills.

Mortally wounded or not, bullies armed with these apparent psychological advantages can take a Matthew Shepard, beat him up, tie him to a fence post, and leave him to die, and when they get arrested, excuse their actions with, "But he was gay." They can take a black man, beat him to death, drag him for two miles behind their pickup, and when arrested, shrug their shoulders and say, "Yeah, but he's black." Topple gravestones in a Jewish cemetery and see it as a fun evening out; torch a mosque and post the video on a website. Trip a boy and sneer as he falls to the ground, "What a klutz!" Text-message an ugly rumor about the new girl, "just because." Swirl a boy's head in a toilet "for laughs—we were just kidding." Humiliating and degrading someone "for the fun of it" has the capacity to permanently pervert a person's normal and natural empathic distress, the natural impetus to reach out and relieve another's suffering. Repeatedly associating pleasure and accomplishment with the infliction of pain makes any future commission of such cruelty easier and the ability to resist such activities more difficult.

In *The Burning Tigris*, Peter Balakian quotes from Aurora Mardiganian's *Ravished in Armenia*, a personal narrative of survival. As one of thousands of Armenian girls raped and thrown into a harem, Aurora describes how the killing squads north of Aleppo in Diyarbekir played "the game of swords" with Armenian girls.

Having planted their swords in the ground, blade up, in a row, at several-yard intervals, the men on horseback each grabbed a girl. At the signal, given by a shout, they rode their horses at a controlled gallop, throwing the girl with the intent of killing her by impaling her on a sword. "If the killer missed," Mardiganian writes, "and the girl was only injured, she would be scooped up again until she was impaled on the protruding blade. It was a game, a contest," the traumatized survivor wrote in her memoir, and after the girls were dead, the Turks forced the Jews of the city to gather up the bodies in oxcarts and throw them into the Tigris River.

Such "sport" can be found in every genocide. It is, indeed, a short walk from the degrading practice of school yard hazing to the "orgies of barbarity" commonly called "initiation activities" in sports clubs, youth groups, and military groups and to the "game of swords." When one finds an imbalance of power, intent to harm, and threat of further aggression, combined with contempt that is propped up with its apparent psychological advantages of a sense of entitlement, liberty to exclude, and intolerance toward differences, along with an experience of pleasure from other human beings' pain, you have the makings of a bullying that is absolutely distinct and a far cry from mere conflict—no matter how deadly that conflict may be.

THE WAYS AND MEANS OF BULLYING

Evil that arises out of ordinary thinking and is committed by ordinary people is the norm, not the exception.
—ERVIN STAUB

There are three kinds of bullying: verbal, physical, and relational. All three can pack a wallop alone, but they are often combined to create a more powerful attack. These are the tools of the *genocidaires*.

1. Verbal Bullying: The adage "Sticks and stones may break my bones but words will never hurt me" is a lie. Words are powerful tools. They create their own consequences. If verbal bullying is allowed or condoned, it becomes normalized and the target dehumanized. Once a person has been dehumanized, it becomes easier to attack him or her without eliciting the normal compassion from those who are within earshot. When a person becomes the regular butt of a joke, he or she is often excluded from other, more prosocial activities—the last to be chosen, the first to be eliminated.

    Verbal bullying can take the form of name-calling, taunting, belittling, cruel criticism, personal defamation, racist slurs, and sexually suggestive or sexually abusive remarks. It can involve extortion, abusive phone calls, intimidating e-mails, anonymous notes containing threats of violence, untruthful accusations, or false and malicious rumors. Of the three types of bullying, verbal bullying is the one that can most easily stand alone and is often the entrée to the other two— that first step toward more vicious and degrading violence—and is even more powerful in combination with the others.

2. Physical Bullying: Although it is the most visible and therefore most readily identifiable form of bullying, it accounts for less than one-third of the bullying incidents reported. It includes, but is certainly not limited to, slapping, hitting, choking, poking, punching, kicking, biting, pinching, scratching, twisting limbs into painful positions, spitting, and damaging or destroying clothes and property belonging to the targeted person. It can easily slip into its more degrading forms: humiliation and torture.

3. Relational Bullying: The most difficult to detect from the outside, relational bullying is the systematic diminishment of the targeted person's sense of self through ignoring, isolating, excluding, or shunning. Shunning, an act of omission, joined with rumor, an act of commission, is a forceful bullying tool. Both are unseen and hard to detect. The person being talked about might not even hear the rumor but will suffer from its effects. Relational bullying can be used to alienate and reject the targeted person. It can involve subtle gestures, such as aggressive stares, rolling of eyes, sighs, frowns, sneers, snickers, and hostile body language. Intentionally excluding is often overlooked as a form of bullying because it is not as readily identifiable as name-calling or a fist in the face; the results are not as obvious as a black eye or a torn jacket; and the pain it causes is usually hidden.

Verbal bullying and relational bullying are the tactics of choice used initially by *genocidaires* and genocidal regimes. Propaganda, rumor, and laws that slowly exclude the targeted group from the social, political, and economic fabric of the society, putting the targeted group outside the web of moral obligation, are preludes, often overlooked for the red flags that they are. These are warnings of worse to come: physical violence, abuse, and finally extermination. Propaganda is also used to elevate the killing of the targeted group to the status of a health necessity or a civic duty.

Goebbels said that taking Jews "out of circulation" was not terror but "social hygiene," in the same way that "a doctor takes a bacillus out of circulation." In November 1992, medical doctor Léon Mugesera—a close friend and confidant of Rwandan President Habyarimana—put out the message that "We the people are obliged to take responsibility ourselves to wipe out this scum ... defend yourselves.... What are we waiting for to decimate these families [of cockroaches]? ... Destroy them. No matter what you do, do not let them get away.... Drive them out. Long live President Habyarimana." On April 20, 1994, President Théodore Sindikubwabo, interim president following Habyarimana's assassination, spoke live on Radio Rwanda from Butare in order to incite the Hutus to get rid of the Tutsis: "Get to work, I authorize it.... What [Prime Minister Kambanda] asked for was done!" Four years after the genocide of the Tutsis in Rwanda, an advisor to the president of the Democratic Republic of the Congo called for the Tutsi "vermin to be eradicated" from the Congo.

RACIST BULLYING: A DOUBLE WHAMMY

The contempt for my people—every assumption,
insult, and slur—was trimmed and tailored for my
infant shoulders before I was born.... It took me
more than thirty years to learn that, unlike being
male or black, being nigger wasn't coded in my
DNA.... I grew up believing that I deserved society's
contempt just because I was black.

—CARL UPCHURCH, *CONVICTED IN THE WOMB:
ONE MAN'S JOURNEY FROM PRISON TO PEACEMAKER*

Racist bullying doesn't just happen. Children have to be
taught to be racist before they can engage in racist bullying.
Racist bullying takes place in a climate where children are
taught to discriminate against a group of people, where
differences are seen as bad, and where the common bonds
of humanity are not celebrated.

Children learn the language of racial slurs and the rules
of bigoted behavior systematically through thought (stereotype), feeling (prejudice), and action (discrimination). First,
children are taught to *stereotype*—that is, to generalize about
an entire group of people without regard to individual
differences: [*Insert group*] are hot-tempered/ugly/filthy/
lazy/stupid/crazy/thieves.

Second, children are taught to *prejudge* a person based
on the stereotype. *Prejudice* is a feeling: We don't like
[Armenians, Jews, Roma, Sinti, Tutsis].

Combine racist thought and feeling, and you get children willing to *discriminate* against individuals in that group.

Racist discrimination morphs readily into scapegoating a particular child or group of children—selecting someone to suffer in place of others or attaching blame or wrongdoing to a specific child when it is not clear who is at fault, and *someone* must be at fault.

The Young Turks, Hitler, and the Hutu Power all scapegoated their intended targets for all of the economic and political woes of their respective countries. Hitler went one step further and was convinced there was an international Jewish conspiracy to take over the whole world. Hitler was not only scapegoating but engaging in a bit of projection as well.

When racist attitudes colocate with the contempt inherent in bullying, they create a deadly combination that enables the *genocidaires* to package their genocidal ideological plans with the pseudo-science of racial hygiene and purity. This type of genocidal ideology was the foundation of all three of the genocides.

A LITTLE ABOUT SEX, A LOT ABOUT CONTEMPT: SEXUAL BULLYING

[Armenian women] were holding hands and walking in a circle slowly, tentatively, as if they were afraid to move. About six Turkish soldiers stood behind them. They had whips and each had a gun. They were shouting, "Dance, *Giaur*. Slut." The soldiers cracked their whips on the women's backs and faces and across their breasts.... Their clothes were now

turning red. Some of them were half naked, others
tried to hold their clothes together ... each crack of
the whip and more of their clothing came off.
—PETER BALAKIAN, *BLACK DOG OF FATE: AN AMERICAN
SON UNCOVERS HIS ARMENIAN PAST*

Just as racist attitudes can collude with bullying, so, too, can
sexist and sexual attitudes. And all three forms of bullying—
physical, verbal, and relational—can be wrapped in sexual
overtones. Because our sexuality is an integral part of who
we are, sexual bullying cuts at the core of our being and can
have devastating consequences, especially for those who are
targeted, but also for the perpetrators and bystanders.

Verbal bullying is the most common form of bullying,
so it makes sense that the most common form of sexual
bullying is verbal. It can stand alone but is often the entrée
to physical sexual bullying or relational sexual bullying,
and is too often the first step toward more vicious and
degrading sexual violence. Verbal bullying can include
threats to sexually violate the target, verbal assessments of
the target's body, sexist or sexual jokes, and derogatory
comments about the target's sexual performance or lack of
sexual activity.

A note about the myth that in male sports clubs or military groups the ritual of reciting lewd, sexualized songs and
jokes is a way to relieve sexual frustration or erotic sexual
feelings. These rituals are not erotic or sexually arousing
and do not relieve sexual frustration. They do something
far more menacing. Such smut coarsens young males' attitudes toward healthy sexual feelings; makes healthy sexual

relations an object of ridicule; objectifies, degrades, and demeans females; expresses control and domination; and makes tenderness something that is "below" them. In a sense, this male "bonding ritual" makes it easier to move on to physical debasement of someone deemed worthless, inferior, or undeserving of respect.

And encouragement toward this kind of debasement comes from other, unexpected sources as well. Actual instructions can be found in writings that all three Religions of the Book (Judaism, Islam, and Christianity) accept as part of their Scriptures. The Book of Numbers tells the story of how God incited Moses to attack the Midianites. Burning all the Midianite cities and slaying all of the men, the soldiers refrained from killing the elderly, the women, and the children. Then Moses gave the order to kill all the boy children and all the women who were not virgins. "But all the women children, that have not known a man by lying with him, keep alive for yourselves" (Numbers 31:18). I don't think "keeping them for themselves" involved a healthy sexual relationship between equals.

Chapter 19 of the Book of Judges tells an equally disturbing story. A Levite traveling with his concubine spent the night in the home of an unnamed "hospitable" man. The men of the city came to the home and demanded that the owner hand over the Levite "so that we may know him." The old man said: "'Nay, my brethren, nay, I pray you, do not so wickedly; seeing that this man is come into mine house do not this folly. Behold, here is my daughter a maiden, and his concubine; them I will bring out now, and humble ye them, and do with them what seemeth good unto you: but unto this man do not so vile a thing'" (Judges 19:23–24). Such male bonding and respect! The story gets worse. The Levite handed over his concubine to the mob, "and they knew her, and abused her all the night until the morning: and when the day began to spring, they let her go. Then came the woman in the dawning of the day, and fell down at the door of the man's house where her lord was, till it was light" (Judges 19:25–26). When she failed to get up as the Levite demanded, he realized she was dead. So he "took a knife, and laid hold on his concubine, and divided her, together with her bones, into twelve pieces, and sent her into all the coasts of Israel" (Judges 19:29). Whether taken as allegories or as literal fact, these words can pack a tremendous wallop; and it would not be the first or last time that intolerance, bigotry, and hatred were cloaked in the garb of religion.

Physical sexual bullying can include, but is certainly not limited to, touching or grabbing in a sexual way, mutilation of sexual parts, stripping, or sexual assault.

Rape is an instrument of genocide. In all three genocides rape was used as a form of terrorism against the targeted community. It was a way to destroy the targeted group and undermine its biological future by "polluting the blood line." Rapes were intended to intimidate, humiliate, and degrade not only the girl or woman raped but also the entire community affected by her rape. It also objectified and dehumanized the women, making it even easier to torture and kill them.

In *Rwanda: Death, Despair and Defiance*, the author writes of the impact of rape, which

> destroys the fundamental fabric and interpersonal relations that constitute a community. It shatters the sense of community and identity of the victim.

Rape isolates a woman from both her family and her community. In addition, the Tutsi women who become pregnant as a result of rape bear children whom they know to be the offspring of the men who so violently violated them.

Many of the women who were raped in all three genocides were tortured before the rape, gang raped, or kept as sex slaves. During the Armenian genocide, U.S. Consul Leslie A. Davis wrote to the American ambassador to the Ottoman Empire, Henry Morgenthau, in Constantinople, describing conditions he observed in the deportation camps:

> [T]he Turks have been taking their choice of these children and girls for slaves or worse. In fact, they have even had their doctors there to examine the most likely girls and thus secure the best ones.

An American missionary in the city of Urfa, the Reverend F. H. Leslie, wrote: "The guards ... were the worst abusers, but also allowed the baser element in every village through which they passed to abduct the girls and women and abuse them."

In Rwanda, the Interahamwe kept large numbers of women in captivity to humiliate, torture, rape, and then kill. Profound consequences follow a genocide, both for the women who were raped and survived, and for the community as a whole. The women are often stigmatized and ostracized. Children born of these rapes are often stigmatized twice—first for being born out of wedlock and then again for being the children of the *genocidaires*. Some are rejected by their mothers and their communities. Others are raised by their mothers but away from family and community, to escape the stigma to both mother and child.

Rape is often the hidden crime of genocide. Even those who have witnessed the aftermath of the killings have often tried to shield from their minds the facts of this crime.

> Since antiquity there was a twisted code of conduct
> that often spared women from direct killing but in
> fact subjected them to even greater misery and agony.
> —R. G. HOVANNISIAN, *THE ARMENIAN GENOCIDE:*
> *A BIBLIOGRAPHY RELATING TO THE*
> *DEPORTATIONS, MASSACRES, AND DISPERSION*
> *OF THE ARMENIAN PEOPLE, 1915–1923*

EXTREME BULLYING: THE EXTRAORDINARY EVIL OF GENOCIDE

> Cruelty is social in its origin much more than it is
> characterological.
> —ZYGMUNT BAUMAN,
> *MODERNITY AND THE HOLOCAUST*

When institutional and situational factors combine with a murderous racial, ethnic, or religious ideology rooted in contempt for a group of people, then bullying is taken to its extreme. The bullies are now well on their way to setting the stage for the dress rehearsals that precede a genocide. What begins as taunting, mocking, hazing, and humiliation quickly progresses to torture, and then on to mass murder. Incinerate children and go home for dinner. Machete to death a baby and matter-of-factly declare, "It's one less cockroach." This behavior arises not from *conflict* or *dispute*, which are susceptible to reason, but rather from contempt—the cold hate that is at the heart of the genocidal impulse.

As a child, Kerop Bedoukian watched "a six-foot Turk, with a two-foot knife in his hand, bargaining with the mother of a fourteen-year-old boy for a price in order not to kill him." Another child heard a Turk bragging about such acts as "tearing a child away from his mother, both screaming in terror."

An eyewitness to massacre in the Armenian village of Moush, German missionary Alma Johannsen described how, after there was no one left in Bitlis to massacre, the Turks turned their attention to her village:

> Cruelties had already been committed, but so far not too publicly; now however, they started to shoot people down without any cause, and to beat them simply for the pleasure of doing so.

She then described the burning of Moush:

> We all had to take refuge in the cellar for fear of our
> orphanage catching fire. It was heart-rending to hear
> the cries of the people and children who were being
> burned to death in their houses. The soldiers took
> great delight in hearing them, and when people who
> were out in the street during the bombardment fell
> dead, the soldiers merely laughed at them.

Her report continued:

> In Kharpert and Mezre the people have to endure
> terrible tortures. They have had their eyebrows
> plucked out, their breasts cut off, their nails torn off;
> their torturers hew off their feet or else hammer nails
> into them just as they do in shoeing horses.

> In his book *Ordinary Men: Reserve Police Battalion 101 and
> the Final Solution in Poland*, Christopher Browning writes
> about battalion commander Major Weis ordering his men
> to comb the Jewish quarter in the city of Bialystok and
> seize male Jews, but not specifying what was to be done
> with them.

> That was apparently left to the initiative of the
> company captains, who had been oriented to his way
> of thinking in the pre-invasion meeting. The action
> began as a pogrom: beating, humiliation, beard

burning, and shooting at will as the policemen drove Jews to the marketplace or synagogue. When several Jewish leaders appeared at the headquarters of the 221st Security Division of General Pflugbeil and knelt at his feet, begging for army protection, one member of Police Battalion 309 unzipped his pants and urinated on them while the general turned his back.

The actions that day quickly escalated to systematic mass murder. Jews were lined up against a park wall and shot. Seven hundred more were burned to death in the town synagogue, with police shooting anyone trying to escape. The next day more than two thousand murdered Jews were taken in thirty wagonloads to a mass grave, with townspeople cheering as the wagons passed.

In Rwanda it was not out of the ordinary to see a group of young men and women singing on their way to their "work" of taunting, torturing, and murdering their neighbors, who had sought refuge in schools, hospitals, and churches. The *genocidaires* often taunted their victims with derogatory racial and sexual epithets before moving on to mutilating and finally killing them. Many Tutsis had the tendons in their feet cut so that they could not flee; family members were forced to watch as their spouses, parents, or children were tortured, beaten, mutilated, or raped in front of them. Victims were thrown alive down into pit latrines and then slowly stoned to death, one rock at a time.

In *Shake Hands with the Devil*, his powerful testimony to the horrors of the genocide in Rwanda, Roméo Dallaire tells of how men, women, and children were rounded up and moved into a church. Priests and officers were seized at the church doors and forced to watch the gendarmes hand the victims over to civilian militiamen:

Methodically and with much bravado and laughter, the militia moved from bench to bench, hacking with machetes. Some people died immediately, while others with terrible wounds begged for their lives or the lives of their children. No one was spared. A pregnant woman was disemboweled and her fetus severed. Women suffered horrible mutilation. Men were struck on the head and died immediately or lingered in agony. Children begged for their lives and received the same treatment as their parents. Genitalia were a favorite target, the victims left to bleed to death. There was no mercy, no hesitation, no compassion.

Genocides don't "just happen." They are methodically executed policies of governments—not spontaneous, unplanned acts of violence, as the Young Turks suggested when forced to explain their attacks on the Armenians during their death march across Anatolia to the Syrian desert of Der Zor. Old men, women, and children were robbed, starved, raped, dehydrated, kidnapped, beaten, and murdered. The Turkish gendarmes either led these atrocities or simply turned a blind eye as marauding youth, trained by the powerful Committee of Union and Progress (CUP), and whole groups of citizens in the towns along the way joined in the violence and seized what was left of the Armenians' meager possessions.

Nor is genocide "the spontaneous outburst of an enraged nation." This was the cause offered by Hitler's press officer, Otto Dietrich, for the well planned, orchestrated, and executed events of November 10, 1938, known as the "Night of the Broken Glass," or *Kristallnacht*, the prequel to the genocide. Supposedly, the German mobs were acting in retaliation for the murder of Ernst von Rath, an official at the German embassy in Paris, by Herschel Grynszpan, a seventeen-year-old Polish Jewish refugee. These mobs, led by local Nazis and armed with lists of names and addresses obviously prepared in advance, destroyed almost one hundred synagogues, burned several thousand others, fire-bombed or otherwise damaged and destroyed eight thousand Jewish businesses, vandalized apartments and homes occupied by Jews, murdered more than a hundred of them and beat and injured hundreds more, rounded up thirty thousand male Jews and sent them to the concentration camps at Dachau, Buchenwald, and Sachsenhausen. Sharing her story with Martin Gilbert in his book *Kristallnacht: Prelude to Destruction*, Miriam Walk said, "The Nazis burned all the books in the streets, and also the Torah scrolls. To this day I feel the stench of the burning and the fear—what next?"

Genocide is also not an act of "sudden irrational lunacy," "the excesses of crowds gripped by fear and ancient hatred," or "justifiable anger of the people." Nor is it "chaotic fighting between warring factions," "uncontrollable tribal killing," or, in the case of Rwanda, "the war with the RPF."

A plane carrying the president of Rwanda, Juvénal Habyarimana, was shot down as it approached the Kigali airport at 8:32 p.m. on April 6, 1994. Within minutes, roadblocks were set up in Kigali and the killing of opposition politicians, dissidents, journalists, and prominent Tutsis began in earnest. Some have insisted that in several sections of Kigali roadblocks were set up as early as 3:30 that afternoon. It was known to the international community that death lists had been drawn up and weapons distributed as early as the previous December.

Genocide is not perpetrated by monsters. To dehumanize the planners, instigators, and perpetrators is to absolve them of personal responsibility, creating "demons" to replace the humans who intentionally, and with great malice, identified and targeted a group of people they deemed worthless, inferior, and undeserving of respect and devised gruesome methods for their extermination. One of the fundamental conclusions of Raul Hilberg's path-breaking study *The Destruction of the European Jews* is that the perpetrators "were not different in their moral makeup from the rest of the population. The German perpetrator was not a special kind of German." They represented "a remarkable cross-section of the German population," and the methods and machinery of destruction they used were "structurally no different from organized German society as a whole."

In his treatise *Reflections*, theologian Thomas Merton wrote about what was, for him, the most disturbing fact to come out in the trial of Adolf Eichmann: "[A] psychiatrist examined him and pronounced him *perfectly sane*. I do not doubt it at all, and that is precisely why I find it disturbing. If all the Nazis had been psychotics ... their appalling cruelty would have been in some sense easier to understand." It would be far more comforting to confirm that they were "mad," "psychotic," or "insane." Then we could safely distance ourselves from such "monsters." In "The Genocide Problem: 'Never Again' All Over Again," genocide scholar and activist Gerry Caplan writes: "It came as no surprise to me that so many well-known, highly reputable genocide scholars subscribe to the old insight memorably articulated by Walt Kelly's sweet comic book character, Pogo Possum: 'We have met the enemy and he is us.' You can't study this subject without wondering about yourself." The safe distance does not exist.

Hannah Arendt spoke of the "banality of evil." It was not the evil that was banal in the extermination of the Armenians, Jews, Roma, Sinti, and Tutsis; it was the banality—the ordinariness—of the people who perpetrated the genocide. Who, then, are these people?

It is not the murderer in Stangle that terrifies us—it is the human being. For that matter "terrify" may not be the right word. Most often one is sick to one's soul. Yes, that is the word needed, a word from Sartre—one is gripped by a profound existential nausea.

—ELIE WIESEL

Chapter 4

Three Characters
and a Tragedy

We used to think that if we knew one, we knew
two, because one and one are two. We are
learning that we must learn a great deal about
"and."

—ARTHUR EDDINGTON, MATHEMATICIAN

The three characters in the tragedy of genocide are the
bully, the bullied, and the bystander. There could be no
genocide without a Talaat, a Hitler, a Hutu Power—the
bullies, the *genocidaires*. But equally they could not have
pulled off what they did without the complicity of
bystanders. Author William Burroughs makes the provocative statement "There are no innocent bystanders," and
then asks the equally provocative question, "What were
they doing there in the first place?" These not-so-innocent
bystanders circle around the bullied—the one who is
targeted. Starting with the bully/bullies on the left side of
the circle, counterclockwise in order of complicity, the
various characters surrounding the target are

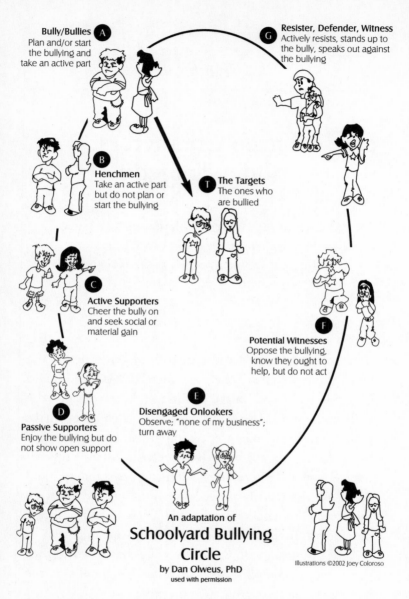

Bully/Bullies A
Plan and/or start the bullying and take an active part

Henchmen B
Take an active part but do not plan or start the bullying

Active Supporters C
Cheer the bully on and seek social or material gain

Passive Supporters D
Enjoy the bullying but do not show open support

Disengaged Onlookers E
Observe; "none of my business"; turn away

Potential Witnesses F
Oppose the bullying, know they ought to help, but do not act

Resister, Defender, Witness G
Actively resists, stands up to the bully, speaks out against the bullying

The Targets T
The ones who are bullied

An adaptation of

Schoolyard Bullying Circle
by Dan Olweus, PhD
used with permission

Illustrations ©2002 Joey Coloroso

For a correlation of the Schoolyard Bullying Circle to genocide, see pages 138–39

A. Bully/Bullies—planners, instigators, and perpetrators, i.e., *genocidaires* who plan, instigate, and/or take an active part in the genocide.
B. Henchmen—who do the Bully's bidding by taking an active part, but do not actually plan or instigate the genocide.
C. Active Supporters—who cheer the Bully on and seek to reap the social, economic, political, and material gain resulting from the policy and procedures of the Bullies.
D. Passive Supporters—who get pleasure from the pain inflicted on the Target by others.
E. Disengaged Onlookers—who watch what happens and say, "It is not any of my business" or "It is a civil war," or cite "ancient animosities"; or turn a blind eye and pretend they don't see; or simply don't take a stand.
F. Potential Witnesses—who oppose the actions of the bullies and know they ought to help those targeted but, for a variety of reasons and excuses, do not act.

This vicious social arrangement makes the killings possible by inviting the merger of role and person that, in turn, creates the capacity for internalizing the evil and shaping later evil behaviors. In other words, each person in the scenario becomes a character actor—someone who specializes in playing the role of an unusual or distinctive character. Slipping into a role offered in the genocide circle, it is easy for the bystanders to become invested in the logic and evil-doing practices of the instigating organization and become not just complicit but "owned by it." In this tight-knit circle, characters find that the more cruel acts they perform, the more it enhances their reputation with the bullies (planners, instigators, and perpetrators) and among their peers. Christopher R. Browning, in *Ordinary Men: Reserve Police Battalion 101 and the Final Solution in Poland*, wrote about the First Company of Police Battalion 61, who were guarding the Warsaw Ghetto: "The company recreation room was decorated with racist slogans, and a Star of David hung above the bar. A mark was made on the bar door for each Jew shot, and 'victory celebrations' were reportedly held on days when high scores were recorded." As this culture of cruelty flourishes, the characters are acting less and less out of obedience and compliance; in fact, they are often initiating and flaunting their own gratuitous and creative cruelties. It is not a fluke that all three genocidal regimes—Young Turks, Nazis, and Hutu Power—introduced programs of nationalist indoctrination and paramilitary training for youth: *Türk Gücü Cemiyeti*, *Hitlerjugend*, and *Impuzamugambi*.

In *Defying Hitler*, Sebastian Haffner's disturbing 1939 memoir chronicling the rise of Nazism, the author, a law candidate, describes the insidious day-to-day changes in attitudes, beliefs, politics, and prejudices that began, for Germans, the slow descent into a "trap of comradeship" in which this culture of cruelty flourished as many of them became "owned by it." "Comradeship," as the Nazis meant it, became a "narcotic" that the people were introduced to from the earliest age, through the Hitler Youth movement

(Hitlerjugend), the SA, military service, and involvement with thousands of camps and clubs. In this way, it destroyed their sense of personal responsibility and became a means for the process of dehumanization:

> It is even worse that comradeship relieves men of responsibility for their actions, before themselves, before God, before their conscience. They do what their comrades do. They have no choice. They have no time for thought (except when they unfortunately wake up at night). Their comrades are their conscience and give absolution for everything, provided they do what everybody else does.

Haffner goes on to describe how this comradeship, in just a few weeks at a camp, molded a group of intellectual, educated men into an "unthinking, indifferent, irresponsible mass" in which bigoted, derogatory, and hateful comments "were commonplace, went unanswered and set the intellectual tone." The Nazis used a variety of psychological stimulations and manipulations to this end, such as slogans, flags, uniforms, *Sieg Heil*s, marching columns, banners, and songs, to help create a dangerous, mindless "group think." One of the most disturbing aspects of this comradeship was how the men in the camp began to behave as a collective entity, who "instinctively ignored or belittled anything that could disturb our collective self-satisfaction. A German Reich in microcosm." This collectivity is the "and" in Arthur Eddington's mathematical formula. The bullies and the bystanders become a deadly combination that is more than the sum of its parts.

However, there is also an "or" that has the potential to radically change this formula. The fourth character, directly across from the bully, the antithesis of the bully, gives us hope that we can break out of this trap of comradeship. This character wears three different and vital garbs—those of the resister, the defender, and the witness. This character is one who will actively resist the tactics of the bully, stand up to the bully, speak out against the genocidal regime, and/or protect, defend, and speak up for those who are targeted. The cycle of violence can be interrupted when even one person has the moral strength and courage to resist the *genocidaires*, defend those who have been targeted, or give witness to the cruelty in order to get it stopped. This character is an awkward and embarrassing reminder that choices are possible, even in the midst of a genocide.

In all three genocides, it was found that if one person (or a small group of dedicated people) refused to go along with the *genocidaires*, some others who were potential witnesses actually became witnesses, defenders, and/or resisters themselves. This group readily admitted that if it were not for those who took the lead in desisting, they probably would not have had the courage to do so themselves. In his research on "atrocity producing situations," Robert J. Lifton came to the conclusion, "There's no inherent human nature that requires us to kill or maim.... We have the potential for precisely that behavior of the Nazis ... or of some kind of more altruistic or cooperative behavior. We

can go either way. And I think that confronting these
extreme situations is itself an act of hope because in doing
that, we are implying and saying that there is an alternative.
We can do better."

> It is immensely moving when a mature man [or
> woman]—no matter whether old or young in years—
> is aware of a responsibility for the consequences of
> his conduct and really feels such responsibility with
> heart and soul. He then acts by following an ethic of
> responsibility and somewhere reaches a point where
> he says: "Here I stand; I can do no other." That is
> something genuinely human and moving.
> —MAX WEBER, "POLITICS AS A VOCATION"

BULLY

> If only there were evil people somewhere, insidiously
> committing evil deeds, and it were necessary only to
> separate them from the rest of us and destroy them.
> But the line dividing good and evil cuts through the
> heart of every human being. And who is willing to
> destroy a piece of his own heart?
> —ALEXANDER SOLZHENITSYN,
> *THE GULAG ARCHIPELAGO*

There are lots of reasons why some people use their abilities and talents to bully other people. No one factor tells
the whole story. Bullies don't come out of the womb as
bullies. Inborn temperament (disposition) is a factor, but so,

too, are what social scientist Urie Bronfenbrenner called "environmental influences": home life, school life, and the community and the culture (including the media) that permit or encourage such behavior. The one thing we know is that bullying is a learned behavior. If it can be learned, it can be examined, and it can be changed.

There are seven kinds of school yard bullies, but for the purposes of this book there are four that tend to be planners and instigators and perpetrators of genocide; the fifth is any combination of these four.

1. The *confident bully* doesn't walk onto the scene; he swaggers onto it, throwing his weight around figuratively and literally. He has a big ego (as opposed to a strong one), an inflated sense of self, a sense of entitlement, a penchant for violence, and no empathy for his targets. He feels good only to the degree that he feels a sense of superiority over others. He is often admired because he has a powerful personality. This does not mean that he has a lot of friends. Friendship is based on trust, loyalty, and mutual respect, not typically characteristics of any bully.

2. The *social bully* uses rumor, gossip, verbal taunts, and shunning to systematically isolate her selected targets and effectively exclude them from social activities. She is jealous of others' positive qualities and has a poor sense of self, but she hides her feelings and insecurities in a cloak of exaggerated confidence and charm.

Devious and manipulative, she can act as if she is a caring and compassionate person, but it is only a guise to cover for her lack of true empathy and a tool to get what she wants. She may be popular, but she is not someone other kids would want to confide in, lest they, too, become a target of her bullying. (Although women played auxiliary roles in the genocide of the Armenians, Jews, Roma, and Sinti, in Rwanda the president's wife, Madame Agathe, had a court within a court called *akazu*, the little house. *Akazu* was the "core of political, economic, and military muscle and patronage" that was to become known as Hutu Power.)

3. The *fully armored bully* is cool and detached. He shows little emotion and has a strong determination to carry out his bullying. He looks for an opportunity to bully when no one will see him or stop him. He is vicious and vindictive toward his target but charming and deceptive in front of others.

4. The *bullied bully* is both a target and a bully. Bullied and abused by adults or more powerful kids, he bullies others to get some relief from his own feelings of powerlessness and self-loathing. Least popular of all the bullies, he strikes out viciously at those who hurt him and at weaker or smaller targets.

5. The *gang of bullies* is a scary lot drawn together not as a group of friends but as a strategic alliance in pursuit of

power, control, domination, subjugation, and turf. Initially joining together to feel a part of a family of sorts, to be respected and to be protected, in their zeal they become so devoted to their group that they disregard their own lives, the carnage they inflict on their targets, and the overall consequences of their actions. Added to this zeal is a lack of empathy and remorse.

It is the gang of bullies, consisting of various combinations of individual bullies, that makes up the regime that plans, instigates, and perpetrates a genocide. Some meticulously plan the genocide but play no other role, standing back and letting others do their dirty work. Some never move beyond the role of instigator and protest at trials that they didn't actually kill anyone. One of the main instigators of the genocide of the Tutsis, Léon Mugesera, declared at his deportation hearing in Canada that he had only written words—hateful and inciting words, but *only* words. In one of his most infamous speeches he exhorted his audience to "rise up" and "exterminate this scum." (In June 2005, the Supreme Court of Canada ordered his deportation and ruled that Mugesera "incited murder, genocide, and hatred." The Court also declared that his speech was in fact a crime against humanity.) Others are originators and instigators and also active perpetrators of the genocide. But they would be unable to do so without having someone to target and bystanders to join in, cheer on, turn a blind eye, or fear the regime.

The road to Auschwitz was built by hatred, but paved
with indifference."

—IAN KERSHAW, "THE PERSECUTION OF THE JEWS
AND GERMAN PUBLIC OPINION IN THE THIRD REICH"

BULLIED

It is true that we Armenians have lost much in these
days of massacre—our men, our women, our children
and our goods. But you Turks have lost more; you
have lost your honour.

—AN ARMENIAN ECCLESIASTIC AT A "RECONCILIATION
BANQUET" HELD AFTER THE 1909 MASSACRE
OF ARMENIANS (A DRESS REHEARSAL
OF SORTS FOR THE GENOCIDE TO COME)

The Armenians, the Jews, Roma, and Sinti, and the Tutsis
all have one thing in common: somebody targeted them for
extermination. Each group was singled out to be the object
of scorn, and thus the recipient of verbal, physical, and relational aggression (bullying), merely because each one of
them was different in some way from those who decided to
target them. Bullies need targets on whom they can heap
their contempt and aggression, and the differences identified as the justifications for these attacks are spurious at
best, contemptuous excuses at worst. The myths that
abound about each one of these targeted groups feed into
the rationalizations that the bullies and bystanders offer for
not putting the responsibility for the bullying on the bully,
for joining in, for turning away from those targeted for

extermination, or, worse, for blaming the targeted group for what is happening to them.

In his last book, *The Drowned and the Saved,* Primo Levi, himself a death camp survivor, wrote a disturbing essay, "The Gray Zone." The "gray zone of *protekcya* [corruption] and collaboration" was to be found in every camp: "That zone of ambiguity that radiates out from regimes based on terror and obsequiousness." Those targeted for extinction often "made pacts with the devil" (the *genocidaires*) in order to stay alive. For Primo Levi, it was the conceiving and organizing of the *Sonderkommandos* (those who stayed alive by running gas chambers and crematoria) that was perhaps one of the worst crimes of the Nazi regime:

> It is naïve and absurd to believe that an infernal system such as National Socialism sanctifies its victims: on the contrary, it degrades them, it makes them resemble itself, and this all the more when they are available, blank, and lacking a political or moral armature.... [T]he time has come to explore the space which separates ... the victims from the persecutors, and to do so with a lighter hand ...

Although the space that separates those targeted and those doing the targeting is a gray zone, the *genocidaires* and their targets may resemble one another but they are not mirror images. Those who were targeted had totally different choices to make, and indeed some were what R. G. Hovannisian has called "choiceless choices," such as the one depicted in the book and film *Sophie's Choice*, in which a woman is forced to choose which one of her children will be killed by the Nazis, and which one will be saved. Other targets have been faced with choosing to leave one child behind on the deportation march when a mother could carry only one of two children across a fast-flowing river; drowning children rather than have them killed by the *genocidaires'* machetes; being forced to choose which child the *genocidaire* could kill in order to save the life of another. And then there were those who themselves were in death camps and were forced to kill family members.

A Jewish officer in the U.S. Army during World War II, Lieutenant Meyer Birnbaum wrote about a young Jewish boy he found near death in Ohrdruff, a concentration camp annexed to Buchenwald. The young boy requested bread and then broke down sobbing as he spoke of his murdered family:

> After about fifteen minutes of bitter sobbing, the sixteen-year-old suddenly looked at me and asked whether I could teach him how to do *teshuvah* [repent]. I was taken aback by his question and tried to comfort him. "After the stretch in hell you've been through, you don't need to worry about doing *teshuvah*. Your slate is clean. Your slate is clean. You're alive, and you have to get a hold of yourself and stop worrying about doing *teshuvah*," I told him. But my words had no effect. I could not convince him. He kept insisting: "*Ich vill tuhn teshuvah*—I

want to do *teshuvah. Ich muz tuhn teshuvah*—I must do *teshuvah.*"

Finally, I asked him, "Why must you do *teshuvah*?" in the hope that talking would enable him to let go of some of the pain I saw in his eyes. He pointed out the window and asked me if I saw the gallows. Satisfied that I did, he began his story:

Two months ago one of the prisoners escaped ... the camp commandant was furious about the escape and demanded to know the identity of the escaped prisoner. No one could provide him with the information he was seeking.... In his fury, the commandant decided to play a sadistic game with us. He demanded that any pairs of brothers, or fathers and sons, step forward. We were terrified of what he might do if we did not comply. My father and I stepped forward.

They placed my father on a stool under those gallows and tied a noose around his neck. Once the noose was around my father's neck, the commandant cocked his Luger, placed it at my temple, and hissed, "If you or your father doesn't tell me who escaped, you are going to kick that stool out from under your father." I looked at my father and told him, "*Zorgst sich nit*—Don't worry, Tatte, I won't do it." But my father answered me, "My son, you have to do it. He's got a gun to your head and he's going to kill you if you don't, and then he will kick the chair out from under me and we'll both be gone. This way at least there's a chance you'll survive. But if you don't, we'll both be killed."

"*Tatte, nein, ich vell dos nit tuhn*—I will not do it. *Ich hab nit fargessen kibbud av*—I didn't forget *kibbud av* [honoring one's father]."

Instead of being comforted by my words, my father suddenly screamed at me: "You talk about *kibbud av*. I'm ordering you to kick that stool. That is your father's command."

"*Nein, Tatte, nein*—No, father, I won't."

But my father only got angrier, knowing that if I didn't obey he would see his son murdered in front of him. "You talk about *kibbud av v'eim* [honoring one's father and mother]," he shouted. "This is your father's last order to you. Listen to me! Kick the chair!"

I was so frightened and confused hearing my father screaming at me that I kicked the chair and watched as my father's neck snapped in the noose.

His story over, the boy looked at me ... as my own tears flowed freely, and asked, "Now, you tell me. Do I have to do *teshuvah*?"

On the subject of those acting in a state of coercion, Primo Levi quotes the nineteenth-century novelist and poet Alessandro Manzoni: "Provocateurs, oppressors, all those who in some way injure others, are guilty, not only of the evil they commit, but also of the perversion into which they lead the spirit of the offended." This does not mean that Levi believes that those who were in a state of coercion did not have any culpability; it is just that if he were forced to judge, "I would lightheartedly absolve all those whose concurrence in guilt was minimal and for whom coercion was of the highest degree."

Mehmed Talaat was assassinated in Berlin in March 1921 by Soghomon Tehlirian, whose family had been killed in the genocide. Soghomon Tehlirian admitted to the killing and was tried in a German court for the murder. The jury took little time to find him not guilty.

It is not uncommon to hear perpetrators try to equate their genocidal behavior with those who killed defending themselves and their families; or with those who, upon arriving in their communities to see their whole family slaughtered, went on a rampage of destruction and killing in a fit of madness and inconsolable grief.

BYSTANDERS

The person who is induced into participation, and who goes far enough in the conversion process so that he or she autonomously and intelligently initiates evil actions, is an individual who has become evil.

—J. M. DARLEY, "SOCIAL ORGANIZATION
FOR THE PRODUCTION OF EVIL"

Bystanders are the third group of players in this story. They are the supporting cast who aid and abet the bullies through acts of commission and omission. They can either stand idly by or look away, or they can actively encourage the bully or join in and become one of the gang of bullies. Whatever the choice, there is a price to pay. Actively engaging with the bullies or cheering them on causes even more distress for the targeted group, encourages the genocidal behavior of the bullies, and puts the bystanders at risk of becoming desensitized to the cruelty, or becoming full-fledged bullies themselves, as was noted in the discussion of the "comradeship trap."

When people in the general population observe the cruel activities of bullies, they are more likely to imitate those activities if they see the perpetrators as popular, strong, and daring role models. It is not uncommon for bystanders to use verbal, physical, and relational denigration of the targeted group to elevate their own status in their "peer" group. The apparent lack of negative consequences, coupled with the bounty of such prizes as elevated status, promotions, approval, and monetary and material rewards for the acts of cruelty, contributes to the breakdown of the bystanders' inner controls against such antisocial activities. Add to these conditions the participation of a *group* of peers—be they neighbors, comrades in arms, police units—and you have a third ingredient: a decreased sense of individual responsibility. The bully is no longer acting alone; the bystanders have become a bunch of bullies who denigrate the targeted group further. This spiraling down equally reduces the guilt felt by the individual and magnifies the negative attributes hung on the targeted group.

The lack of sanctions for the genocidal acts, the breakdown of inner controls, the reduction of feelings of guilt, and the magnification of the targets' negative attributes all contribute to the cultivation of a world view that reinforces the stereotypes, prejudices, and discrimination that are part and parcel of the genocidal ideology. This in turn hinders bystanders from responding with empathy, sympathy, or compassion for the human beings who are being taunted, isolated, tormented, or slaughtered.

Standing idly by or turning away each has its own costs. In his comments on the French Revolution, author François-René de Chateaubriand wrote a caustic note to those who think standing idly by is an acceptable course of action: "Such neutrality is derisory for it works against the weaker party and plays into the hands of the stronger party. It would be better to join forces with the oppressor against the oppressed for at least that would avoid adding hypocrisy to injustice." Injustice overlooked or ignored becomes a contagion that infects even those who thought they could turn away. The self-confidence and self-respect of the bystanders are eroded as they wrestle with their fears about getting involved and with the knowledge that to do nothing is to abdicate their moral responsibility to those who are targeted. One can imagine the hopelessness and desperation of those who are being publicly tormented, and who feel that hopelessness and desperation compounded by the knowledge that those who observed their humiliation and spoke not a word of protest or raised a hand to stop it have abandoned them. The cruelty of genocide is riveting to watch but distressing to contemplate. No one is left untouched.

The question that begs to be asked is this: Why would so

many people who would not instigate this cruelty be willing to become a part of the attack or turn a blind eye to the plight of the targeted? There are a few valid reasons and lots of excuses.

The four valid reasons most often given for not intervening follow:

1. The bystander is afraid of getting hurt or being killed. The bully is bigger, stronger, and has a reputation that justifies the fear, so jumping in to stop the cruelty does not appear to be a smart thing to do.
2. The bystander is afraid of becoming a new target of the bully. Even if the bystander is able to intervene successfully, there is a chance that he or she will be singled out at a later date for retribution. Bullies are quick to disparage and malign anyone who tries to intervene.
3. The bystander is afraid of doing something that will only make the situation worse for both the target and the bystander.
4. The bystander does not know what to do.

As legitimate as they are, these reasons do not shore up the self-confidence or self-respect that is eroded when a bystander witnesses the cruelty done to the target and is unable or unwilling to respond effectively to stop the cruelty. All too often these fears and lack of skill turn to apathy—a potent friend of contempt. Contempt grows best in a climate of indifference.

Bystanders have more excuses than valid reasons for not intervening. These excuses help poison the social environment, increasing the likelihood that bystanders will side with the bullies and eventually assume the role of bullies themselves. They include but are certainly not limited to these seven:

1. *The bully is my comrade.* Bystanders are less willing to intervene if the bully belongs to the same political party, same group, or same clique.

2. *It's not my problem!* Socialized not to interfere in other people's affairs, to do their own work, and to look out for number one, bystanders can excuse themselves by claiming to be minding their own business. This is also known as indifference. In her prologue to *Rescuers: Portraits of Moral Courage in the Holocaust,* Cynthia Ozick writes of the danger inherent in such an excuse: "Indifference finally grows lethal ... the act of turning away, however empty handed and harmlessly, remains nevertheless an act."

3. *The target is not in my circle of concern.* Bystanders are more willing to intervene when the person targeted fits into their circle of concern. One of the first things the *genocidaires* do is exclude the target group from their circle of concern by dehumanizing them.

4. *The target deserved to be attacked, asked for it, had it coming. Why stop something that is warranted? They didn't even stand up for themselves, so why should anyone else stand up for them?* This excuse appears to get the

bystanders off the hook, but it fails to take into account the basic principle that bullying is about contempt. No one deserves to be stripped of dignity and self-worth. Targeted groups cannot act alone to successfully fend off a genocidal gang of bullies intent on exterminating them.

5. *Who wants to be called a snitch or a rat, blamed for getting someone else in trouble?* The bystanders abide by a deeply imbedded code of silence. What isn't considered in this excuse is the immorality of silence in the face of malice.

6. *It's better to be in the in-group than to defend the outcasts.* In a genocidal clique, once the leaders identify the targeted group, the rest of the group tends to fall mindlessly into line, doing the bullies' bidding without much consideration for the rights and feelings of the outcasts ("comradeship trap"). The in-group becomes so tightly connected and single-minded that there is no room for protest, dissent, or differences. The need for approval and acceptance within even a genocidal clique is so strong that even if the bystander felt the momentary urge to protest the harm being done to the target group, that urge would be quickly squelched. When such cliques are the norm, as they are in all genocides, there is a clear demarcation of "us," "them," and "those below us and them," thus deserving of contempt and not worthy of concern.

7. *It's too big a pain in the brain.* A bystander must weigh the pros and cons of remaining faithful to the group

versus siding with the targeted group. This mental calculation can create tremendous emotional tension—especially at the beginning of the genocide. The fastest way to reduce the tension is to magnify the pros of marching lockstep with the group and magnify the cons of helping the targeted group. Add the four legitimate reasons above to excuses number one through six and the answer is simple—don't get involved—or, better yet, join in with the bullies. Added bonus: the headache is gone. Standing up, speaking out, and getting involved to help the targeted group can be complicated, risky, difficult, painful, and/or lethal.

Taken together, these reasons and excuses contribute to the erosion of civility and compassion. When civility is diminished, it is replaced by a false sense of entitlement, an intolerance toward differences, and a liberty to exclude, all of which allow bullies and their accomplices to harm the targeted individuals without feeling empathy, compassion, or shame. But how can a small group of genocidal bullies engage whole communities in the wholesale slaughter of family members, neighbors, friends, and coworkers? The engagement involves more than these reasons and excuses, more than the three apparent psychological advantages: moral inhibitions must be broken down.

Evil is not simply the result of a decision to do a bad thing; it is refusing to do a good thing.
—STEPHEN L. CARTER, *INTEGRITY*

MORAL INHIBITIONS

It was constantly impressed upon me in forceful terms that I must obey promptly the wishes and commands of my parents, teachers, and priest, and indeed all grown-up people, including servants, and that nothing must distract me from this duty. Whatever they said was always right. These basic principles by which I was brought up became second nature to me.

—RUDOLPH HOESS, COMMANDANT AT AUSCHWITZ

Far more, and far more hideous, crimes have been committed in the name of obedience than have ever been committed in name of rebellion.

—C. P. SNOW

Having grown up Jewish in anti-Semitic Vienna, spent a year under Nazi rule and another year as a refugee in Antwerp, and escaped to the United States just before Germany's invasion of Belgium, Herbert Kellman has spent most of his adult life researching the source of unquestioning obedience and the source of principled resistance to unjust authority, the two polar opposites that characterize, respectively, the various henchmen and other bystanders, on one hand, and the defenders, resisters, and witnesses, on the other. As a social psychologist and professor of social ethics at Harvard, Kellman said: "We can learn more by looking, not at the motives for violence, but at the conditions under which the usual moral inhibitions against violence can be weakened." In his book *Crimes of Obedience*, Kellman identifies these conditions leading to genocide:

1. Unquestioning obedience to authority that relieved the killers of personal responsibility;
2. Routinization of cruelty that turned the commission of violence into a normal operation; and
3. Dehumanization, in which a group of people are stripped of their humanity, their personal identity, and any connection to the community.

1. UNQUESTIONING OBEDIENCE TO AUTHORITY THAT RELIEVED THE KILLERS OF PERSONAL RESPONSIBILITY

Unquestioning obedience to authority enables bullies to get their accomplices to carry out their dirty work. It is this same obedience that enables genocidal regimes (a gang of bullies) to carry out their extermination plans. Once individuals surrender themselves to being obedient to an authority, they are absolved of the responsibility to make moral choices of their own regarding the situation. As well, Kellman explains that "when acts of violence are explicitly ordered, implicitly encouraged, tacitly approved, or at least permitted by legitimate authorities, people's readiness to commit them or condone them is readily enhanced."

In the Ottoman Empire, a young soldier used these words to explain how he helped carry out the genocide of the Armenians without any thought for the people he was murdering: "I am a soldier, [the nation] is my commander—I obey without question all its orders—with closed eyes I carry out my duty." It was not only soldiers who obeyed without question in the genocide of the Armenians. With a respect for authority that was partially rooted in Islam, and partially rooted in the authoritarian government and patriarchal family structure, the masses saw their Sultan as a spiritual and secular leader, a father figure to be obeyed.

In Germany, every member of the Hitler Youth movement learned and recited the Commandments of the National Socialists. The message was clear: questioning the authority of the leader was out of the question.

The Commandments of the National Socialists

The Leader is always right!

Never violate the discipline!

Never waste your time with idle talk, with self-complacent critique, rather use your hands and accomplish something!

Be proud but not conceited!

Let the program be your dogma; it demands your total dedication to the movement!

You are a representative of the party, be guided accordingly in your behavior and appearance!

Let loyalty and unselfishness be your highest command!

Exercise faithful camaraderie, then you are a true Socialist!

Treat your fellow Germans as you would like to be
     treated!
In the struggle be tough and secretive!
Courage is not rudeness!
Right is what benefits the movement and therefore
     Germany, which means your fellow Germans!
If you act according to these commandments, then
     you are a true fighter for your Leader.

Toward the end of the war, as the Nazis were being
defeated, Dr. Joseph Goebbels spoke at a rally and
reminded the war-weary Germans that the regime would
emerge victorious from the current crisis. He told the
crowd to "have blind faith in victory! This is not only a
matter of courageous hearts and the determination of our
souls! This is a matter of unconditional obedience and
loyalty to our Führer!" The crowd responded with loud
applause and long shouts of *"Heil Hitler."*

In Rwanda, people looked to the government for solutions to their problems, and in return they followed orders.
François Xavier Nkurunziza is a Kigali lawyer who escaped
death by moving from one hiding place to another.
Speaking to Philip Gourevitch, author of *We Wish to Inform
You That Tomorrow We Will Be Killed with Our Families*, he
explained that conformity and obedience to authority are
deeply rooted in Rwandan culture and history. This rever-
ence for power, along with a lack of education, played into
the government's hands:

You take a poor, ignorant population and give them arms, and say, "It's yours. Kill." They'll obey. The peasants, who were paid or forced to kill, were looking up to people of higher socio-economic standing to see how to behave. So the people of influence, or the big financiers, are often the big men in the genocide. They may think that they didn't kill because they didn't take a life with their own hands, but the people were looking to them for their orders. And in Rwanda an order can be given very quietly.

Nkurunziza described two kinds of obedience, which Kellman defines: obedience because of the *rule*, and obedience because of the *role*. Rwandan peasants often obeyed because they had learned to obey any *rule* that was handed down by the authority that provided solutions to their problems. The peasants' tasks were to "follow the rules, respect authorities' demands, do what is required of them, and stay out of trouble." They were often compliant, and performed cruel acts to avoid sanctions from authority. Those of higher socio-economic status for the most part obeyed because of the *role* they played in the government, their desire to perceive themselves as good citizens "who meet their role obligations by actively supporting the government and faithfully obeying its demands." They identified with the authority and could be counted on to be enthusiastic about carrying out their duties. (For example, Adolf Eichmann didn't just do his job, he did it with enthusiasm and zeal, making sure those trains to the death camps ran efficiently and on time.)

2. ROUTINIZATION OF CRUELTY THAT TURNED THE COMMISSION OF VIOLENCE INTO A NORMAL OPERATION

Once the authorization process is in full swing and people become involved in actions without making any decisions (following orders), and without reflecting on the implications of those actions (unquestioning obedience), they find themselves in social situations that, in a sense, take on a life of their own. The inhibitions that might have kept them from taking the initial steps into cruel and criminal acts are removed once they obediently cross the line. Once that line is crossed, those performing the acts now seek ways to become more involved, in an effort to justify the actions and avoid negative consequences. They will also aggressively try to get others to participate so that "we are all in this mess together," and no one will have clean hands. Once the *genocidaires* have routinized and normalized cruelty, it is easier to mobilize entire communities to become involved in what has become the norm—torturing, raping, pillaging, and killing.

Routinization also involves sanitation of language. Killing becomes "final solution," "evacuation," "trimming the trees," "killing the cockroaches," "collecting cabbage," "special treatment," "finding a new home," "relocation." For those participating in the atrocities, such as "collecting cabbage"—delivering severed heads of Tutsis to the commander—the use of such language enabled them to cover up, even in their own minds, the literal reality of the killing of another human being.

As I have already mentioned, humiliating and degrading someone "for the fun of it" has the potential to permanently pervert a person's normal and natural empathic distress. Repeatedly associating the infliction of pain with pleasure and accomplishment makes any future commission of such cruelty easier, and the ability to resist such activities more difficult. Not only did the perpetrators in all three genocides cross over the line, covering up their deeds with euphemisms, they often went about their business singing and whistling, at times jeering their victims and cheering their comrades. They also received accolades for their "accomplishments"—"career" advancement, a portion of the pillaged goods, monetary compensation—which in turn created a greater incentive to continue the cruelty.

3. DEHUMANIZATION, IN WHICH A GROUP OF PEOPLE ARE STRIPPED OF THEIR HUMANITY, THEIR PERSONAL IDENTITY, AND ANY CONNECTION TO THE COMMUNITY

Josias Semujanga writes in *Origins of the Rwandan Genocide:*

The probability of genocide tends to be around zero as long as all members of society recognize the quality of humanity. Conversely, if a human group is considered less than human, genocide becomes highly probable. For, once the campaign of demonization of the "other" reaches its high point among the majority, the bureaucratic organization of genocide becomes a question of means.

Stripping their targets of their humanity through verbal, relational, and/or physical bullying, bullies intend to make their targets feel unworthy of respect, isolated, and shamed. In a genocide, people who are slaughtered are targeted for killing merely because of who they are, not what they have done. Labels, tattooed numbers, and laws help to deprive them of their own identity and their place in the community. *Genocidaires* terrorize, starve, and denigrate their targets. The conditions the targeted group are forced to exist in only reinforce the process of dehumanization. As they begin to look less and less like healthy human beings, it becomes easier for their tormentors to treat them as less than human beings, and to see them instead as "cattle," "filthy dogs," "cockroaches," "vermin," "rats."

In a September 10, 1916, letter to Jesse Jackson, the American consul in Aleppo, Syria, German businessman Auguste Bernau wrote of the horrors he had witnessed on his journey across Armenian encampments, noting that the Armenians were "brutally dragged out of their native land ... penned up in the open like cattle." He went on to describe Armenian men, women, and children eating "herbs, earth and even their excrement." When he gave them bread they "threw themselves on it like dogs dying of hunger, took it voraciously into their mouths with hiccups and epileptical tremblings."

In *Night*, Elie Wiesel describes a forced march in Buchenwald.

> The SS made us increase our pace. "Faster, you tramps, you flea-ridden dogs.... Faster, you filthy dogs." We were no longer marching, we were running. Like automatons. The SS were running as well, weapons in hand.... The night was pitch-black. From time to time, a shot exploded in the darkness. They had orders to shoot anyone who could not sustain the pace. Their fingers on the triggers, they did not deprive themselves of the pleasure. If one of us stopped for a second, a quick shot eliminated the filthy dog.

In his memoirs, the SS Commandant of Auschwitz comments that the inmates at the concentration camp "are not like you and me. You saw them yourself; they are different. They look different. They do not behave like human beings."

From the sixteenth century on, the Ottoman Empire was a theocratic state based on Islamic precepts. The Empire was a plural society with "believers" (Muslims) and "nonbelievers" (Jews and Christians) living and working side by side, yet separate and distinct. Nonbelievers were called by the pejorative term *"gavurs,"* meaning "infidels."

But in the nineteenth century, in spite of their status (rein-
forced by laws) as *"rayahs"* (a pejorative term meaning, literally, "cattle"; a euphemism for second-class citizens), Jewish
and Christian Armenians enjoyed religious and cultural
autonomy within the Ottoman Empire. As the Empire
declined, however, and experienced the depressed aftermath of its defeat in the Caucasus, the anti-Armenian
measures began. Armenians were now no longer just
"rayahs"; they became "the Armenian Problem." And as a
"problem," they were no longer considered within the
Turks' moral circle of concern.

In January 1915, Armenian soldiers and gendarmes were
disarmed and placed into work brigades, then taken in small
groups to remote areas and executed. Just as retaliation for
the murder of Ernst von Rath provided an excuse for
Kristallnacht, the Night of the Broken Glass, and the incur-
sion by the RPF was used as an excuse to attack civilian
Tutsis, the resistance of the Armenians of Van was used as
the pretext for the beginning of mass arrests of the
Armenian intelligentsia and deportations of the rest of
the Armenian population. (Just as in the other genocides,
the mass arrests and deportations—euphemistically called
"relocations"—had begun before the event in Van. The
excuse came after the fact and provided "cover" for an
escalation of those actions.)

In actuality, the Young Turks had written a detailed script
for the genocide as early as December 14, 1914. Vahakn N.
Dadrian analyzed the following document in his treatise
"The Secret Young Turk Ittihadist Conference and the

Decision for the World War I Genocide of the Armenians." Subtitled "The Ten Commandments of the Committee of Union and Progress," it is a verbatim translation of a document issued at a conference presided over by Mehmed Talaat Pasha and by Drs. Mehmed Nazim and Behaeddin Shakir (masterminds of the Special Organization, responsible for carrying out the massacres).

The Ten Commandments of the Committee of Union and Progress

1. Profiting by the Arts: ... close all Armenian Societies, and arrest all who worked against the government at any time among them and send them into the provinces such as Baghdad or Mosul, and wipe them out either on the road or there.
2. Collect arms.
3. Excite Moslem opinion by suitable and special means, in places as Van, Erzeroum, Adana, where as a point of fact the Armenians have already won the hatred of the Moslems, provoke organized massacres as the Russians did at Baku.
4. Leave all executive to the people in the provinces such as Erzeroum, Van, Mamuret ul Aziz, and Bitlis, and use Military disciplinary forces (i.e., Gendarmerie) ostensibly to stop massacres, while on the contrary in places as Adana, Sivas, Broussa, Ismidt and Smyrna actively help the Moslems with military force.

5. Apply measures to exterminate all males under 50, priests and teachers, leave girls and children to be Islamized.

6. Carry away the families of all who succeed in escaping and apply measures to cut them off from all connection with their native place.

7. On the ground that Armenia officials may be spies, expel and drive them out absolutely from every Government department and post.

8. Kill off in an appropriate manner all Armenians in the Army—this is to be left to the military to do.

9. All action to begin everywhere simultaneous, and thus leave no time for preparation of defensive measures.

10. Pay attention to the strictly confidential nature of these instructions, which may not go beyond two or three persons.

So, too, had Hitler written the script for the genocide of the Jews. In his speech of January 30, 1939, he once again spoke as he had in 1920 of an open threat of a mass murder.

I have often in my lifetime been a prophet and have been mostly derided. At the time of my struggle for power it was in the first instance the Jewish people who only greeted with laughter my prophecies that I would someday take over the leadership of the state and of the entire people of Germany and then, among other things, also bring the Jewish problem to its solution. I believe that this hollow laughter of the Jewry in Germany has already stuck in its throat. I want today to be a prophet again: if international finance Jewry inside and outside Europe should succeed in plunging the nations once more into a world war, the result will be not the Bolshevization of the earth and thereby the victory of Jewry, but the annihilation of the Jewish race in Europe.

Before Hitler put the final touches on his script, the stage was being set with various laws designed to disenfranchise the Jews. And what became known as the Nürnberg laws resulted from a direct order by Hitler on September 13, 1935. The two laws promulgated at the Reichstag in Nürnberg on September 15, 1935, and the First Regulation to the Reich Citizenship Law of November 14, are usually included in what is known as the Nürnberg Laws.

The Reich Citizenship Law of September 15 says, in part,

(1) A Reich citizen is only that subject of German or kindred blood who proves by his conduct that he is willing and suited loyally to serve the German people and the Reich.
(2) Reich citizenship is acquired through the conferment of a certificate of Reich citizenship.
(3) The Reich citizen is the sole bearer of full political rights as provided by the laws.

The Law for the Protection of German Blood and German Honor, passed on the same day, says, in part,

> Imbued with the insight that the purity of German blood is a prerequisite for the continued existence of the German people and inspired by the inflexible will to ensure the existence of the German nation for all times, the Reichstag has unanimously adopted the following law, which is hereby promulgated:

> 1. (1) Marriage between Jews and the subjects of German or kindred blood are forbidden. Marriages nevertheless concluded are invalid, even if concluded abroad to circumvent this law.
>   (2) Only the State Attorney may initiate an annulment suit.
> 2. Extramarital intercourse between Jews and subjects of German or kindred blood is forbidden.
> 3. Jews must not employ in their households female subjects of German or kindred blood who are under 45 years old.
> 4. (1) Jews are forbidden to fly the Reich or national flag and to display the Reich colors.
>   (2) They are, on the other hand, allowed to display the Jewish colors. The exercise of this right enjoys the protection of the state.

Other laws were soon to follow. All of these not only dehumanized Jews but also contributed to the routinization of cruelty as they removed Jews from any active involvement in German society. On October 14, 1937, the SS journal *Das Schwartz Korps* declared that Jewish business should "disappear," or in other words, be confiscated. In January 1938 an internal memo of the government required the removal of all poor Jews for "economic reasons." On April 22, 1938, a law was passed forbidding the "hiding" of the identity of Jewish businesses; June 25, 1938, Jewish doctors were prohibited by law to treat non-Jewish patients; August 17, 1938, all Jewish females were required to add "Sarah" to their names and Jewish males the name "Israel"; September 27, 1938, German Jews were barred from practicing law; October 5, 1938, all Jewish passports were required to be marked with the letter "J." This not only identified a Jew in Germany but also enabled other countries to more readily identify a Jew and therefore limit the number of Jews immigrating. By January 1, 1939, Jews could be employed only by a Jewish organization.

In a diary entry for November 2, 1941, Dr. Joseph Goebbels conveys the ideology of dehumanization that was perpetrated at the height of the Nazi regime:

Here the Jews crouch among one another, horrible forms to see, not to mention touch.... The Jews are the lice of civilized humanity. They have to be exterminated somehow; otherwise, they will again play their tormenting and annoying role. Only if one proceeds against them with the necessary brutality will we be finished with them. When you spare them, you subsequently become their victim.

Fifty years later, borrowing from the infamous anti-Semitic forgery known as *Protocols of the Elders of Zion*, Hitler's *Mein Kampf,* and the Nürnberg Laws, and combining those ideas with aspects of Rwandan mythology turned on their head, Hutu Power created the doctrine of "The Hutu Ten Commandments," reinforcing the stereotype of Tutsi men as power-hungry, wicked, deceitful, and an enemy to be destroyed, and Tutsi women as *"femmes fatale."* The manifesto was published in December 1990 in *Kangura,* a journal sponsored by leading extremists.

The Hutu Ten Commandments

1. Every Muhutu should know that a Mututsi woman, wherever she is, works for the interest of her Tutsi ethnic group. As a result, we shall consider a traitor any Muhutu who:
   a. Marries a Tutsi woman;
   b. Befriends a Tutsi woman;
   c. Employs a Tutsi woman as a secretary or a concubine.
2. Every Muhutu should know that our Hutu daughters are more suitable and conscientious in their role as woman, wife, and mother of the family. Are they not beautiful, good secretaries and more honest?
3. Bahutu women, be vigilant and try to bring your husbands, brothers and sons back to reason.
4. Every Muhutu should know that every Mututsi is dishonest in business. His only aim is the supremacy

of his ethnic group. As a result, any Muhutu who does the following is a traitor:

a. makes a partnership with Batutsi in business;

b. invests his money or the government's money in a Tutsi enterprise;

c. lends or borrows money from a Mututsi;

d. gives favors to a Batutsi in business (obtaining import licenses, bank loans, construction sites, public markets, etc.).

5. All strategic positions, political, administrative, economic, military and security should be entrusted to Bahutu.

6. The education sector (school pupils, students, teachers) must be majority Hutu.

7. The Rwandese Armed Forces should be exclusively Hutu. The experience of the October [1990] war has taught us a lesson. No member of the military shall marry a Tutsi.

8. The Bahutu should stop having mercy on the Batutsi.

9. The Bahutu, wherever they are, must have unity, solidarity, and be concerned with the fate of their Hutu brothers.

a. The Bahutu inside and outside Rwanda must constantly look for friends and allies for the Hutu cause, starting with their Bantu brothers;

b. They must constantly counteract the Tutsi propaganda;

    c. The Bahutu must be firm and vigilant against their common Tutsi enemy.

10. The Social Revolution of 1959, the Referendum of 1961, and the Hutu Ideology, must be taught to every Muhutu at every level. Every Hutu must spread this ideology widely. Any Muhutu who persecutes his brother Muhutu for having read, spread and taught this ideology, is a traitor.

Borrowing the traditional cadence of Rwandan song, this manifesto was to be the foundational document of the genocidal propaganda against the Tutsis. Commandment Eight was often chanted as the *genocidaires* marched off to their "work": "The Bahutu should stop having mercy on the Batutsi."

THESE THREE CONDITIONS—unquestioning obedience to authority, routinization of cruelty, and dehumanization of a targeted group—help to set the stage for genocide and provide a necessary backdrop. Any time these three conditions exist in a society, a gang of bullies in positions of power can walk on with their genocidal script, get all the characters to rehearse, and raise the curtain on the first act.

Kellman defined a third kind of obedience: *value orientation*. People whose obedience is based on value orientation are committed to their government "because they share the cultural and institutional values on which they believe the state to be founded." They don't merely obey; they take an active role in formulating, evaluating, and questioning the policies of the state. Just as in the other genocides, it was the politicians, journalists, and human rights workers—those who questioned and challenged the Hutu Power government in Rwanda—who were seen as a grave threat to the genocidal regime and were some of the first to be killed on April 6 and 7, 1994.

Peasants whose ethic (way of being in the world) was grounded in a deep caring (loving-kindness and compassion) for themselves and for their neighbors, and people of higher economic status who had that same deep caring and a concern for the "state of the nation" were the ones who defended, resisted, and gave witness in all three genocides—often at the cost of their own lives. These people are a threat to a genocidal regime because, even in the face of routinization of cruelty and the dehumanization policies and procedures, their moral inhibitions against violence remain strong. In fact, resisters, defenders, and witnesses are often energized by railing against such cruelty and inhumanity, growing even more daring, more convicted, more resourceful, and more committed to rescuing those whom the regime has targeted for extermination.

Jaap Penraat, an architect and industrial designer who saved 406 Jews in the Nazi-occupied Netherlands by forging false documents and personally taking many people, masquerading as construction workers, to safe haven, spoke of his deeds as "doing the decent thing. You do these things because in your mind there is no other way of doing it." In his early twenties, as a part of a resistance movement, he put his design talents to use making false identity cards, and spent a few months in jail when he was discovered. His story, told in Hudson Talbott's children's book *Forging Freedom: A True Story of Heroism During the Holocaust*, chronicles his daring adventures. In researching the story, Talbott found what he called "a daredevil aspect to the missions.... [Jaap Penraat] just loved the idea of putting one over on the Nazis. It wasn't a joke, or a game, but clearly there was something about fooling them that was an important aspect of this."

> We must make up our minds. Neutrality favors the oppressor, never the victim. Silence encourages the persecutor, never the persecuted.
>
> —ELIE WIESEL

DEFENDERS, RESISTERS, AND WITNESSES

> Whoever saves a single life is as one who has saved the entire world.
>
> —MISHNAH SANHEDRIN 4:5

Those who refused to obey the orders of the authorities, and come to the aid of persecuted people, were neither saints nor heroes. Rather their goodness was that of ordinary men and women who were responsive to the victims' manifest need for help. The way they acted was part of their everyday life, and they did not perceive it as something extraordinary. They did not feel like heroes at the time, nor do they want to be seen as such in retrospect.

—F. ROCHAT AND A. MODIGLIANI, "THE ORDINARY
QUALITY OF RESISTANCE: FROM MILGRAM'S
LABORATORY TO THE VILLAGE OF LE CHAMBON"

In the three genocides, the *genocidaires* tried to eliminate defenders, resisters, and witnesses—anyone who might threaten the political monopoly of the *genocidaires*, interfere with the control of information and propaganda, or muster any resistance against the exterminations. In Rwanda, in the first few days after the downing of the president's plane, many of those targeted for death were prominent politicians, senior civil servants, wealthy businesspeople with ties to the political opposition, journalists, and human rights activists. Political moderates and their supporters were a special threat to the ideology of the extremists. They had the potential to expose and oppose that ideology and collectively break the hold the regime had on the entire government system.

Control of information and of the media was critical for inciting the populace and for the dissemination of misinformation, propaganda, and lies to the international community. Up to this point, censorship and harassment had been unable to muzzle journalists entirely—their death was seen as the only absolute "solution." Human rights activists monitored, documented, and denounced human rights abuses, offered support to those targeted by the regime, collaborated with the independent press to report the abuses, and worked with international human rights groups. They were very visible in their communities and were unmercifully targeted, mocked, and tortured before being killed.

There were those who refused to obey the orders of a corrupt government, who stood up for the targets of the genocides and fought injustice, no matter the cost. Defenders, resisters, and witnesses confound and disturb those who are unquestionably obedient to a diabolical regime. What is the makeup of people who are willing to speak out against injustices or risk their lives to rescue those whom their neighbors set out to destroy? Why are they willing to heed the call for help when the rest of humanity turns a blind eye? How do they, often at great cost to themselves, use their imagination and intellect to create at times complicated schemes to save one person, or hundreds? Do the initial acts of courage also change the person doing the act? Most important: What can we learn from them?

Giving proof of the existence of good and the possibility of defiance of the perceived inevitability of the genocidal impulse, people of all ages on every continent have refused to violate their own ethic—their way of being in the world—and have done the right thing, simply because it was the right thing to do. Almost all had a tendency to care deeply, share generously, and help willingly, and, most important, to be inclusive with these tendencies—to include in their circle of caring those belonging to a different social, ethnic, or religious group. Just as repeated acts of cruelty strengthened and helped perpetuate acts of cruelty, so, too, did repeated acts of courage and bravery strengthen and perpetuate those acts of kindness and daring. Those who resisted, defended, and gave witness to the suffering of those who were targeted by the *genocidaires* often stated that they were changed by their own actions. And even if the deeds were done initially out of duty, from a sense of obligation, to help a relative or friend, or simply because they were asked to help, in the end their actions were motivated by a *must* to relieve someone else's suffering.

In *The Roots of Evil*, Ervin Staub writes of the power of defenders and how their actions have affected others. In the Huguenot village of Le Chambon in Vichy, France, the people

> saved several thousand Jews, mostly children, despite a penalty of deportation or death for sheltering Jews. Their pastor, André Trocme, who had a firm belief in nonviolence and the sanctity of life, led them. Their willingness to sacrifice themselves had a great impact even on would-be perpetrators, such as the police and the military. It became common for strange voices to call on the telephone in the presbytery to tell of an impending raid. This enabled the inhabitants to send the refugees they were harboring into the nearby forest.

When Nazis invaded Denmark in 1940, citizens of all ages united to form a strong resistance movement. Refusing to cooperate with the planned deportation of Jews, the Danes began spiriting their neighbors and relatives across the channel to Sweden in small fishing vessels. Scientists and fishermen worked together to come up with ways to numb the noses of the dogs used by the Nazis to search these vessels for stowaways. The small boats, with their undetected human cargo, met up with larger Swedish ships in the channel. In all, 7,200 of the 7,800 Danish Jews and 700 of their non-Jewish relatives were smuggled safely out of Denmark.

One of those resistance workers, seventeen-year-old Preben Munch-Nielson, from a small fishing village, wrote an account of this daring rescue and explained why he and the many other Danes defied the Gestapo:

> You can't let people in need down. You can't turn the back to people who need your help. There must be some sort of decency in a man's life and that wouldn't have been decent to turn the back. So there's no question of why or why not. You just did. That's the way you're brought up. That's the way of tradition in my country. You help, of course ... could you have retained your self-respect if you knew that these people would suffer and you had said, "No, not at my table"? No. No way. So that's not a problem— you just have to do it. And nothing else....
>
> There must be some sort of decency in a man's life and that wouldn't have been decent. So there is no question of why or why not. You just did. That's the way you were brought up.

Just as courageous was a young German naval attaché, Georg Duckwitz, who leaked in advance to the Danes the Germans' plan for the deportation of Jews. Georg Duckwitz committed this act of conscious disobedience to save lives, willing to accept whatever penalties might be imposed as a consequence. So, too, was the Hutu informant code-named Jean-Pierre, who warned General Roméo Dallaire of the impending genocide, providing him with names of key instigators in the genocidal regime, locations of weapons caches, lists of people who were marked to be killed, and an outline of the planned attacks. All he asked in return was safe harbor for himself and his family. The United Nations denied Dallaire's request and reminded him that he must remain *neutral*, *impartial*, and *act only with the consent of the involved parties*. Jean-Pierre disappeared. His fate is unknown.

Taken from a wall on resistance at the Ghetto Fighters' House in Israel is a litany of ways people resisted *genocidaires* and their henchmen.

To smuggle a loaf of bread was to resist.
To teach in secret was to resist.
To cry out warning and shatter illusions was to resist.
To rescue a Torah scroll was to resist.
To forge documents was to resist.
To smuggle people across borders was to resist.
To chronicle events and conceal the records was to resist.
To hold out a helping hand to the needy was to resist.

> To contact those under siege and smuggle weapons
> was to resist.
> To fight with weapons in streets, mountains, and
> forests was to resist.
> To rebel in death camps was to resist.
> To rise up in ghettos, among the crumbling walls, in
> the most desperate revolt was to resist.

People talk about the Armenians, the Jews, and the Tutsis going meekly to their death, not resisting, behaving as sheep being led to the slaughter. The facts contradict this myth. It is true that some believed the lies that said they were merely being relocated "for their own good"; others, thinking it was "just" one more pogrom (official, organized persecutions or massacres of a minority group), failed to see the more ominous signs. Still others, after being relentlessly targeted, humiliated, separated from the larger community, and tortured, did go to their deaths with resignation—death being a relief. And some, in order to survive or save themselves and their families from instant death, colluded, cooperated with, or reluctantly allied themselves with the *genocidaires*, hoping against hope for a reprieve.

In all three genocides, individuals struck back, resisted, and defended others. Those who were being targeted reached out individually to help those who were suffering with them. Genocide survivor and psychiatrist Viktor Frankl wrote, in *Man's Search for Meaning*, about such people: "We who lived in concentration camps can remember those who walked through the huts comforting others, giving away their last piece of bread." Pierre Vidal-Naquet, writing in the preface to *A Crime of Silence: The Armenian Genocide: Permanent Peoples' Tribunal*, tells of Armenians saved from death by the American missions and the Apostolic Nuncio. Others were rescued by "the resolute intervention by Turkish officials, or had been hidden by Kurdish or Turkish friends."

There were major uprisings and strong resistance, but in each case the *genocidaires* were more numerous, had better weapons, and could outlast those who so bravely resisted.

French scholar Yves Ternon, in his report to the Permanent Peoples' Tribunal at the session on the genocide of the Armenians held in Paris in 1984, wrote:

> In the Jebel Musa, or Musa Dadh, the Armenians refused to submit to the deportation order issued on 13 July [1915]. Retreating into the hills they took up a strategic position and organized an impregnable defense. The Turks attacked and were repulsed by huge losses. They proceeded to lay siege to the Jebel Musa with fifteen thousand men. Fifty-three days later, French and British ships, intercepting signals, picked up the four thousand survivors and took them to Port Said.

There were also cases of resistance in Urfa, Shabin-Karahisar, and Van.

Between 1941 and 1943, many Jews in ghettos across Eastern Europe tried to organize armed groups to resist the Germans. It was in the Warsaw ghetto in January of 1943 that the most famous armed resistance began to fight back against the Germans' attempt to deport more Jews to the death camp Treblinka. The Germans retreated after a few days. Inspired by their success against the heavily armed Germans, the resisters, known as Z.O.B. and led by twenty-three-year-old Mordecai Anielewicz, prepared to resist any further deportations. On April 19, 1943, what came to be known as the "Warsaw Ghetto Uprising" began as German troops and police once again attempted to deport the remaining Jews. Seven hundred and fifty fighters were able to hold out against the heavily armed Germans until May 16, 1943. At that point, Germans captured 56,000 Jews, shot 7,000 in the ghetto, and deported the rest to the death camps.

From April until June 1994, 50,000 Tutsis in Bisesero, armed with only clubs and spears, fought back against soldiers, policemen, militia, trained Interahamwe fighters, and civilians equipped with grenades and guns, who were supported by wealthy businessmen providing financial incentives as well as equipment and supplies. When word spread of the brave and determined resistance, soldiers and militia poured in from various prefectures, along with a large number of the Presidential Guard, vowing to kill every last Tutsi on the hill. From May 13 on, the refugees were killed by the tens of thousands. In fact, in just two days, it was believed that half of the refugees were killed.

By late June, only about 2,000 emaciated people were still alive. These few survivors risked coming out of their hiding places to call for help from

French reconnaissance troops who were driving by on 26 June as part of Operation Turquoise. The French troops promised to return in three days. In the meantime, the Interahamwe, anxious to destroy the evidence of their crimes, set out to murder every last survivor. They had killed nearly 1,000 of them by the time the French soldiers, alerted by a foreign journalist, returned to organize their evacuation.

There were those who thought at first they could do the most good working within the system, but they came to realize that this was absolutely wrong. Dr. Martin Niepage, a teacher at a German school in Aleppo during the Armenian genocide, wrote of how he was dissuaded by the head of the school, Director Huber, from resigning his post in protest against the horrors around him:

> It was pointed out to me that there was value in our continued presence in the country, as eye witnesses of what went on. Perhaps, it was suggested, our presence might have some effect in making the Turks behave more humanely towards their unfortunate victims, out of consideration for us Germans. I see now that I have remained far too long a silent witness of all this wickedness.

There were those who paid with their lives for reaching out to help. When the Central Committee of the CUP sent out telegrams ordering the annihilation of the Armenians, some refused, such as the Prefect of Midyat, who was murdered for his defiance. Some Muslims and Kurds who hid Armenians were hanged and their homes burned. Hutus who tried to protect their neighbors or friends—or even their own spouses who were Tutsis—were killed along with the Tutsis. A young Hutu gave witness in criminal trials, giving voice to those who were dead and forcing those who killed them to admit to their vicious and cruel attacks on children. He was killed when he returned to his community.

Others were penalized. A Swiss engineer was court-martialed for distributing bread in Anatolia to the starving Armenian women and children in a convoy of exiles. A Polish woman, Antonina Wyrzykowska, was ostracized from her community after rescuing seven Jews.

Others put themselves at great risk to aid and defend those who were targeted or to give witness for them. The first president of the American Red Cross, Clara Barton, mobilized sophisticated relief teams to the Armenian provinces of the Ottoman Empire. Harvard-educated Varian Fry, forging passports and finding secret paths across the Pyrenees, during thirteen months in 1940 and 1941 led one of the most successful private rescue missions of World War II.

Armin T. Wegner, a German nurse and second lieu-tenant in Field Marshal von der Goltz's command, violated orders and photographed the atrocities committed against Armenians, giving the world irrefutable evidence of the slaughter.

Viscount James Bryce, at one time Great Britain's ambassador to the United States, described the beginnings of the genocide in an account published in *The New York Times* on September 21, 1915:

> Accounts from different sources agree that over the whole of Eastern and Northern Asia Minor and Armenia the Christian population is being deliberately exterminated, the men of military age being killed and the younger women seized for Turkish harems, compelled to become Mohammedans, and kept, with the children in virtual slavery. The rest of the inhabitants, old women, men, and children, have been driven under convoy of Turkish soldiers into unhealthful parts of Asia Minor, some to the desert regions beyond the Euphrates. Many die or are murdered en route, and all perish sooner or later.

Viscount Bryce wrote about what he personally witnessed: "In Trebizond City, where the Armenians numbered over 10,000, orders came from Constantinople to seize all Armenians. Troops hunted them, drove them to the shore, took them to sea, threw them overboard, and drowned them all—men, women, and children."

The American ambassador at Constantinople from 1913 to 1916, Henry Morgenthau, wrote *Ambassador Morgenthau's Story*, a first-person account that was to become one of the central sources of documentation on the genocide. He brought the scope and intensity of the genocide to the world's attention. In his July 16, 1915, telegram to the U.S. Secretary of State, Morgenthau pleaded for intervention.

> Deportation of and excesses against peaceful Armenians is increasing and from harrowing reports of eye witnesses it appears that a campaign of race extermination is in progress under a pretext of reprisal against rebellion.
>
> Protests as well as threats are unavailing and probably incite the Ottoman government to more drastic measures as they are determined to disclaim responsibility for their absolute disregard of capitulations and I believe nothing short of actual force which obviously the United States are not in a position to exert would adequately meet the situation. Suggest you inform belligerent nations and mission boards of this.

Morgenthau was engaged, as were large numbers of the public, and the press. But the paralysis that the ambassador alluded to in regard to national politicians was at the same time palpable ("I believe nothing short of actual force which obviously the United States are not in a position to exert would adequately meet the situation"). Some people who worked on the German-run Baghdad railway protected Armenians; others stood by as cattle cars were loaded with Armenians. In England there was strong public reaction, led by the Opposition leader, William Gladstone, but the policymakers feared Czarist Russia and thus courted Turkey. In his suicide note, Polish Jew Szmul Zygielbojm lamented that "by passive observation of this murder of defenseless millions and of the maltreatment of children, women, and old men, these countries have become the criminals' accomplices.... I was unable to do anything during my life; perhaps by my death I shall contribute to destroying the indifference of those who are able and should act." Roméo Dallaire was to face the same passivity and paralysis, from the United Nations as a whole and member states in particular, while at the same time witnessing courageous and heroic acts by ordinary human beings.

The man who translated for me The Commandments of the National Socialists from the *Handbook for Hitler's Youth*, Rudi Florian, was a member of the group for a short period of time. "In 1944 at the age of ten I joined the Hitler Youth, the *Jungvolk*. This was the Hitler Youth's equivalent to the Cub Scouts. More Nazi indoctrination followed, but thanks to my parents, the poison affected me very little. After attending only about five meetings of our group, I had had enough of it and was looking for a way out. My mother came to my rescue and provided me with a perfect excuse: I had to babysit my younger sister. The group leader came a few times to our home inquiring about my whereabouts and my mother used the same excuse every time until he grew tired of hearing and finally stayed away. That was the end of my career in the Hitler Youth."

It was in 1947 that he saw a documentary on the genocide of the Jews in a movie theater in East Berlin. He was shocked that his own people could have committed such a horrible crime. "This question weighed heavily on my mind and still does. I felt betrayed by those I had looked up to as my mentors and role models, and I was deeply ashamed. I also resented very much this 'conspiracy of silence' that kept me in the dark." Reading everything he could, he pledged he would do his part to warn that this could happen again, anywhere.

The authors of the African Rights text *Rwanda: Death, Despair and Defiance* wrote of the many defenders, resisters, and witnesses of the genocide of the Tutsi, but they could have just as easily been writing about any of the other genocides when they described the many ways that the people of Rwanda helped each other to survive and to hold on to their humanity during a terrifying time

> when all they could foresee was the triumph of mass murder. Not knowing which values would be vindicated, their actions were undertaken from humanity and principle alone.

Just as there is ordinariness about those who commit extraordinary evil, there is an ordinariness of those who commit extraordinary goodness. By studying the words and actions of those who not only did not succumb to the intoxicating madness around them, but also railed against it, we can begin to see a way out of the morass of contempt, a way to rewrite the script, to create new roles, and write ourselves a different ending.

Life and study have persuaded me of the openness of history. There is no inevitability in history. Thinking about what might have happened, what could have happened, is a necessary element in trying to understand what did happen. And if, as I believe, individual acts of decency and courage make a difference, then they need to be recorded and remembered. We deem the future in a free society, however constrained by pre-existing conditions, to be open, and if this is so, then the civic engagement also becomes a moral and political imperative.

—FRITZ STERN, *THE FIVE GERMANYS I HAVE KNOWN*

Chapter 5

The Bully Circle

The historical evidence on the spontaneity,
inventiveness, and enthusiasm with which the
Nazis degraded, hurt, and killed their victims
also argues against explaining their behavior as
simply responses to authority's commands
despite the perpetrators' abhorrence toward their
own actions, and without hate toward their
victims. It must have come from within ...

—LEONARD S. NEWMAN, RALPH ERBER,
EDITORS, *UNDERSTANDING GENOCIDE*

When speaking to educators, I use the Bully Circle (see page 82), from *The Bully, The Bullied, and the Bystander,* to demonstrate in graphic form the manner in which the three characters (bully, bullied, and bystander) act in relation to one another and play a part in bullying. When I was asked in 2005 to speak at the University of Rwanda in Butare on the topic, I could not merely lecture on bullying in the school-yard. During the genocide, the university had been "cleansed" of its Tutsi population. Since so many staff and students had been killed on that campus eleven years before,

I decided to use the 2005 lecture as an opportunity to show how it was a short walk from schoolyard bullying to criminal bullying (hate crime) to genocide. It was the three characters in the tragedy and the schoolyard Bully Circle that got the students to engage in the conversation about the genocide that had ravaged their country. They already knew that what had happened was something very different from a *conflict*, with only two characters going at each other. Using the language of bullying, they quickly identified various players in this tragedy by name and role. Marking up the Bully Circle, without much hesitation, they were able to assign a place (or places) on the circle to individuals, groups, institutions, nations, and the United Nations. Word spread, and during the rest of my stay in Rwanda I watched in utter amazement as survivors, witnesses, lawyers in the Department of Justice, the Youth minister, senators, and reporters, individually and in groups, related events in their various communities, and in the country as a whole, using the Bully Circle as a starting point. There were heated discussions when it came to designation of individuals, countries, institutions, churches, the United Nations, UNAMIR, and the French initiative Operation Turquoise: Where did they fit? Was it possible to play several roles simultaneously? And, even more perplexing, was it possible to be both a henchman and a defender?

One survivor told me of her husband being murdered by neighbors, after which she and her children sought refuge in a convent, where her sister and her children were all turned away. She told me about a soldier who refused to join with the *genocidaires*, saying he was fighting a war against the RPF, not against all Tutsis. That same soldier ordered nuns, at gunpoint, to shelter men, women, and children in the new section of the convent, where it was safer. Another survivor told me of being exposed as a Tutsi by one Hutu classmate at a roadblock, while another Hutu classmate gave him money to pay his way into the shelter of the Hôtel Des Mille Collines, where more than a thousand people took refuge. He told me about priests giving their lives to help rescue Tutsis, while others affiliated with the Church participated in the killings. A member of the RPF talked about the heroism of some children who, at ages nine and ten, willingly hid and fed Tutsis, while others the same age led the *genocidaires* to the hiding places of Tutsis.

It was physician and senator Odette Nyiramilimo who talked to me about the question of whether it is possible to be both a henchman and a defender. She told me about a man who had shown mercy to her children during the genocide, but she said she felt no warmth for him. This man had willingly participated—with fervor and unspeakable cruelty—in the killing of other children. It was not uncommon for some who killed many and rescued a few to try to use those few they rescued as a "get out of jail free card," as if the one or two times they rescued someone would somehow exonerate them of the multiple crimes they committed. But to Odette—and other survivors I spoke with—the fact that these *genocidaires* saved some people only proved that they could not be judged innocent, since it demonstrated plainly that they knew killing those other Tutsis was wrong. Could there be any hope that they might feel true remorse for their crimes? Showing mercy for one child might suggest some empathy and compassion for those targeted and not saved, and perhaps remorse for killing them, but not necessarily. There are many less-magnanimous reasons for rescuing one or two while slaughtering the rest. Some acted with *seeming* kindness only, the overt act masking the covert intent of greed.

There were others who did indeed rescue many and felt tremendous grief and remorse for killing those they were forced to murder. According to many survivors, in a case documented by African Rights, a thirty-seven-year-old Hutu mother of six was a reluctant murderer. When she was taken to the office of the local commune, the wounded were shown to her, and it was indicated which one she was expected to "finish off." She refused to kill. Because of this, she was beaten with rifle butts so severely that her two-month-old baby—a girl who she carried on her back— was killed. Some Hutus were forced to kill family members. One man was told to kill his two children, "who were considered to have the mother's Tutsi looks."

As Shakespeare said, "one man in his time plays many parts," which makes the issue even more complicated. It is possible to move from one role to another—from potential witness to witness, resister, and/or defender, as Oskar Schindler did during the Holocaust—or to move from the role of potential witness to active supporter, henchman, or instigator, as did some of the men of Police Battalion 101 in Poland. The more one does good, the easier it becomes to do more good. The more one acts cruelly, the easier it is to be cruel again. There are those who were forced to kill and those who died refusing to kill. *Rwanda: Death, Despair and Defiance* documents hundreds of acts of courage and compassion that testify to the strength of human values in the face of evil and moral disorientation. "The extremists' propaganda presented an alternative morality, and the attacks on the churches and hospitals sought to cut people adrift from the certainties that anchored their sense of right and wrong." The killers made killing the norm, aware that a society will generally accept what is "normal" as what is "right." But in the midst of this "alternative morality" there were men and women, old people and young children—people of decency and tremendous courage—who resisted the killings.

I have since shared the Bully Circle with family members of survivors of the genocide of the Armenians, and survivors of the genocide of the Jews. Just as those who survived the genocide of the Tutsis were able to place various individuals and groups as well as countries on the circle, these people had no trouble assigning roles and telling stories related to each character. Telling their own stories was often much harder.

Hasmig Kurdian wrote for me her father's story of surviving the genocide to include in this book. Before she told his story, she related, "I brought up the subject with my mother (who is now 94, but with the heart and brains of a smart young woman). She was quite moved, as I expected. I asked her to retell me my father's adventure as a young boy, so as to pass on a better picture. It is strange that details were not discussed with us children at home: maybe to protect us? I remember my maternal grandmother used to say 'I want to pray, but as soon as I utter the first few words of "The Lord's Prayer," I see the long lines of deportees and my children whom I lost on the way and I can't go on.'"

Though we want to believe that violence is a matter
of cause and effect, it is actually a process, a chain in
which the violent outcome is only one link.

—GAVIN DE BECKER, *THE GIFT OF FEAR*

COMPLICITY OF BYSTANDERS

Injustice anywhere is a threat to justice everywhere.
We are caught in an inescapable network of mutual-
ity, tied in a single garment of destiny.

—MARTIN LUTHER KING, JR.,
LETTERS FROM BIRMINGHAM JAIL

As much as many *genocidaires* protest that they were only
doing what they were ordered to do, didn't really want to
engage in the degrading and murderous activities, would
have stood up if they could have, and feel bad about what
they did, the facts don't often bear such protestations
out. The following texts are cited at length to debunk
this common myth and to demonstrate, in each genocide,
the genocidal ideology and contempt of the instigators, the
complicity of the many, and the great decency and extraordinary courage of a few.

The first text is from Kersam Aharonian, who was born
on November 9, 1916, on the deportation route from his
parents' native Zeitoun to the Syrian deserts. The words in
parentheses identify the place on the Bully Circle occupied
by each of the actors identified in the account:

It is true the ultimate responsibility for the plan to deport and exterminate the Armenian people lies with the Turkish leadership **(planner, instigator, perpetrator)**. But can anyone say that the "Turkish people" raised their voices **(witness, resister, defender)** against the inhuman decisions of their leaders? Did the Turkish public condemn **(witness)** the hellish verdict announced by their leaders? No one can present proof of this. On the contrary, there is evidence that ordinary Turkish citizens everywhere applied themselves with unprecedented fervor to the task of perpetrating the genocide **(henchmen, active supporters)**. The Turks dishonored and tormented the Armenian women **(targets)** with an indescribable and unquenchable sadism. Young Armenian boys and girls **(targets)** were made the victims of immoral practices. The Turks **(planner, instigator, perpetrator)** invented unimaginable forms of torture and then observed with immense pleasure **(active bystanders/passive bystanders)** the torment of their victims. Dissatisfied with the state of starvation of those who had been deported, they **(henchmen)** dehumanized them to their sadistic gratification. The murder of young children **(targets)** by the usual means did not satisfy them, so they loaded them on boats and had them dumped into the sea near Trebizond. Other innocent children **(targets)** were cut to pieces with knives. Thousands of others were taken to the desert to live like dogs. This is what the

monster Zeki **(instigator, perpetrator)** did in Der
Zor. Such acts of brutality were committed by the
thousands, and the Turkish people **(henchmen,
active supporters/passive supporters)** enjoyed and
were satisfied with what was done.

Eighty-nine-year-old   Armenian   survivor   Zakar
Berberian shared his story with Robert Fisk in Beirut in
1992:

I was twelve years old in 1915 and lived in Balajik on
the Euphrates.... What I saw on the day the Turkish
gendarmes **(henchmen)** came to our village I will
never forget. I had not yet lost my eyesight.... The
men **(targets)** were ordered to leave the village—they
were taken away and never seen again. The women
and children **(targets)** were told to go to the old
market. The soldiers **(henchmen)** came in and in
front of their mothers, they picked up each child
(target)—maybe the child was six, seven, or eight—
and they threw them up in the air and let them drop
on the old stones. If they survived, the Turkish
soldiers picked them up again by their feet and beat
their brains out on the stones.... The Turkish soldiers
were in uniform **(henchmen)** and they had the
gendarmerie of the government **(henchmen)** with
them.... The Turks **(henchmen)** tied one of my
friends **(target)** by his feet to the tail of a horse and
dragged him out of the village until he died.

There was a Turkish officer **(defender, witness)** who used to come to our shop. He sheltered my brother **(target)** who had deserted from the army but he said we all must flee, so we left Balajik for the town of Asma. We survived then because my father **(target)** changed his religion. He agreed to become a Muslim. But both my father and my mother got sick. I think it was cholera. They died and I was sick and like a dead person. The deportations went on and I **(target)** should have died but a Turk **(defender)** gave me food to survive.

Berberian was eventually taken to an orphanage:

They **(defender)** gave me **(target)** a bath but the water was dirty. There had been children **(targets)** in the same bath who had glaucoma. So I bathed in the water and I too went blind. I have seen nothing since. I have waited ever since for my sight to be given back to me. But I know why I went blind. It was not the bath. It was because my father changed his religion. God took revenge on me when we forsook him.

The third is the testimony given in the deposition of Szmul Wasersztajn, who witnessed the humiliation, degradation, torture, and killing of almost all the Jews in the Polish town of Jedwabne. He gave witness before the Jewish Historical Commission in Bialystok on April 5, 1945:

Before the war broke out, 1,600 Jews **(targets)** lived in Jedwabne, and only seven survived, saved by a Polish woman, Wyrzykowska **(witness, defender)**, who lived in the vicinity.

On Monday evening, June 23, 1941, Germans **(instigators, perpetrators)** entered the town. And as early as the 25th local bandits **(henchmen)**, from the Polish population, started an anti-Jewish pogrom. Two of those bandits, Borowski (Borowiuk?) Wacek with his brother Mietek **(active supporters)**, walked from one Jewish dwelling to another together with other bandits **(active supporters)** playing accordion and flute to drown the screams of Jewish women and children **(targets)**. I **(witness)** saw with my own eyes how those murderers **(henchmen)** killed Chajcia Wasersztajn, Jakub Kac, seventy-three years old, and Eliasz Krawiecki **(targets)**.

Jakub Kac **(target)** they **(henchmen)** stoned to death with bricks. Krawiecki **(target)** they **(henchmen)** knifed and then plucked his eyes and cut off his tongue. He suffered terribly for twelve hours before he gave up his soul.

On the same day I **(witness)** observed a horrible scene. Chaja Kubrzanska **(target)**, twenty-eight years old, and Basia Binsztajn **(target)**, twenty-six years old, both holding newborn babies **(target)**, when they saw what was going on, they ran to a pond, in order to drown themselves with the children rather than to fall into the hands of the bandits **(henchmen)**. They put

their children in the water and drowned them with
their own hands: then Baskka Binsztajn jumped in
and immediately went to the bottom, while Chaja
Kubrzanska suffered for a couple of hours. Assembled
hooligans **(active supporters)** made a spectacle of
this. They advised her to lie face down in the water so
that she would drown faster. Finally seeing that the
children were already dead, she threw herself more
energetically into the water and found her death too.

The next day a local priest **(passive supporter
intervening only to allow Germans to do the
"dirty work")** intervened, explaining that they should
stop the pogrom, and that the German authorities
(instigators) would take care of things by themselves.
This worked, and the pogrom was stopped. From this
day on the local population **(active supporters)** no
longer sold foodstuff to Jews **(targets)**, which made
their circumstances all the more difficult. In the
meantime rumors spread that the Germans **(instigators)** would issue an order that all the Jews **(targets)**
be destroyed.

Such an order was issued by the Germans **(instigators)** on July 10, 1941.

Even though the Germans **(instigators)** gave the
order, it was Polish hooligans **(henchmen)** who took
it up and carried it out, using the most horrible
methods. After various tortures and humiliations,
they **(henchmen)** burned all the Jews **(targets)** in
the barn. During the first pogrom and the later

bloodbath the following outcasts distinguished them-
selves by their brutality: Szlezinski, Karolak, Borowiuk
(Borowski?) Mietek, Borowiuk (Borowski?) Waclaw,
Jermalowski, Ramutowski Bolek, Rogalski Bolek,
Szelawa Stanislaw, Szelawa Franciszek, Kozlowski
Geniek, Trzaska, Tarnoczek Jerzyk, Ludanski Jurek,
Laciecz Czeslaw **(instigators/henchmen)**.

On the morning of July 10, 1941, eight Gestapo
men **(instigators)** came to town and had a meeting
with the representatives of the town authorities **(insti-
gators/henchmen)**. When the Gestapo **(instigators)**
asked what their plans were with the Jews **(targets)**,
they **(instigators)** said, unanimously, that all Jews
must be killed. When the Germans proposed to leave
one Jewish family from each profession, local carpen-
ter Bronislaw Szezinski **(instigator)**, who was present,
answered: We have enough of our own craftsmen, we
have to destroy all of the Jews, none should stay alive.
Mayor Karolak **(active supporter)** and everybody
else **(active supporters)** agreed with his words. For
this purpose Szlezinski **(instigator)** gave his own
barn, which stood nearby. After this meeting the
bloodbath began.

Local hooligans **(henchmen)** armed themselves
with axes, special clubs studded with nails, and other
instruments of torture and destruction and chased all
the Jews **(targets)** into the street. As the first victims
of their devilish instincts they **(henchmen)** selected
seventy-five of the youngest and healthiest Jews

(targets), whom they ordered to pick up a huge monument of Lenin that the Russians had erected in the center of town. It was impossibly heavy, but under the rain of horrible blows the Jews (targets) had to do it. While carrying the monument, they (targets) also had to sing until they brought it to the designated place. There, they were ordered to dig a hole and throw the monument in. Then these Jews (targets) were butchered to death and thrown into the same hole.

The other brutality was when the murderers (instigators/henchmen) ordered every Jew (targets) to dig a hole and bury all previously murdered Jews, and then those were killed and in turn buried by others. It is impossible to represent all the brutalities of the hooligans (instigators/henchmen) and it is difficult to find in our history of suffering something similar.

Beards of old Jews (targets) were burned, newborn babies (targets) were killed at their mother's breast, people (targets) were beaten murderously and forced to sing and dance. In the end they (instigators/hench-men) proceeded to the main action—the burning. The entire town was surrounded by guards (active supporters) so that nobody could escape; then Jews (targets) were ordered to line up in a column, four in a row, and the ninety-year-old rabbi (target) and the *shochet* [Kosher butcher] (target) were put in front, they were given a red banner, and all were ordered to sing and were chased to the barn. Hooligans **(hench-men)** bestially beat them up on the way. Near the gate a few hooligans **(active supporters)** were standing, playing various instruments in order to drown the screams of horrified victims. Some **(targets)** tried to defend themselves, but they were defenseless. Bloodied and wounded, they were pushed into the barn. Then the barn was doused with kerosene and lit, and the bandits **(henchmen)** went around to search Jewish homes, to look for the remaining sick and children **(targets)**. The sick people they found they carried to the barn themselves, and as for the little children, they roped a few together by their legs and carried them on their backs, then put them on pitchforks and threw them onto smoldering coals.

After the fire they **(henchmen)** used axes to knock golden teeth from the still not entirely decomposed bodies and in other ways violated the corpses of holy martyrs **(targets)**.

The fourth account is found in a letter from Hasmig Kurdian, a granddaughter and daughter of survivors of the genocide of the Armenians. She shared in her letter to me the continuing trauma of her maternal grandmother from the death of her children in the forced march, and the resilience and tenacity of her father.

The fifth account is from a letter written to me in the summer of 2006 by Isaie Munyaneza, a survivor of the genocide of the Tutsis, as he prepared to give testimony against the killers of his family and other relatives. I will leave it to the reader to identify the characters in these two powerful personal statements.

My Father, who was born in 1907, must have been 7 or around 8 when the Armenians from Erzrum (northeastern Turkey now) were deported. We know from our maternal Grandmother that they walked six months to get to Mosul in northern Iraq.

My Father, named Katchpérouni at his birth, lost all his family members. The last one he lost was his sister who was kidnapped in Mosul. In Iraq he was grabbed by an Arab shepherd, who took him home. My Father's duty was to look after the goats. Every evening, after dinner (!), they used to make him pray with them, but when he went to his sleeping mat, he covered his head, made the sign of the cross and repeated his name.

One day, quite alert as to what was happening around him, he overheard his new "parents" [say] that they were going to make him a Muslim officially (maybe that meant circumcision?). He sensed danger and the next day, after he took the herd to the pasture, he left the goats and took the road that led to Mosul. How did he know that? Well, merchandise was transported along that route.

As he had nothing to eat, he traded the Arabian fez that he had for a handful of raisins. He hid in daylight, and continued his walk in the dark.

Finally he got to Mosul. There he inquired where the Church was (necessity is the mother of creativity and alertness too). It happened to be a Saturday, and there is service on Saturday evenings.

Some women from his hometown, among whom [was] a distant relative, recognized him. The woman took him to her dwelling, then, when AGBU [Armenian General Benevolent Union] organized the gathering of orphans across the Middle-Eastern countries, he was taken to an orphanage in Basra.

From there he, along with other children, was moved to the orphanage in Jerusalem, and then to Lebanon. He later left the orphanage with a close friend (though young for their age) to go to the orphanage in Aleppo, learn a craft and move to the newly declared independent state of Armenia and make his home there—a dream that did not come true.

The change in his name (to Khathig) happened when he started working. His original name was hard to pronounce for Arabs. I still have my parents' wedding permit (not license) which carries his original name.

My father did not have much schooling, but he was an avid reader. He read anything he could get hold of in Armenian. My brothers used to call him a walking encyclopedia of Armenian and world geography and history. What could have become of him if he had had a normal childhood!

Life Was Useless for Tutsis in Rwanda During the Genocide
(Isaie's Testimony)

The morning of April 7th, 1994, Mum asked me if I knew what was going happen to us. I was very surprised and I immediately realized that Mum was completely annoyed. I asked her how it was and she informed me that Habyarimana Juvénal, the President of the Republic, was killed. She continued telling me that it was a complete plan for killing the Tutsis that we are. I randomly felt fear in my heart, but I told Mum that the Interahamwe (killers) could not kill us because there were a lot of [UN-UNAMIR] soldiers. Mum gathered us all and told us what was going on. After almost thirty minutes Dad came. He looked completely discouraged and afraid. Some neighbors came home and we talked about what happened in our country and the local leaders ordered every old person to go to attend the meeting. In the meeting they said that the Goverment ordered all people to check whether no percolators or Cockroach (RPF soldiers) reached our village. "What we can do is to put a lot of barriers on all strategic places," they continued saying. When we were at the meeting, we saw at the next sector called "Musha" where the bureau of the District was, the people were burning the Tutsis' houses and killed them, too. All the people of my village [were] convinced that they could not kill any person so, all the people that could had to make a hard patrol to offense the killers from the district.

In the village, there was a police station of [Gendarmerie Nationale] which was in charge of securing the electricity cabin. They were eight policemen. Two of them came and went with two representatives of people for the security reasons. Two hours later, the two representatives who went with the policemen came and told us, "Every person has to go home and no one is allowed to leave his house and you have to wait for new regulations." Really in my village the people were in good collaboration; some Hutus went to the Tutsis and talked all about the meeting of the police and leaders. It was a recommendation from the highest leaders to exterminate all Tutsis, one neighbor told Dad. The Tutsis got informations about them and we took a conclusion to take refuge to the next sector which was at least safe.

The next day, the Tutsis and some moderate Hutus (who did not want the war) went across the valley not far from my home, trying to escape with important materials and food going to the next hill called Bwana. The dwellers of this hill were not convinced to kill the Tutsis.

In the evening, almost at 18.00 p.m, all the Tutsis who stayed in the village were killed and among them one young man called "Jean de Dieu Nyirigira" tried to escape, but he had been hurt and wounded on his hand by a machete. At the same time, the Interahamwe gathered and set our houses on fire using petrol. We were watching them because it was next to the hill where we hid. That night, the Interahamwe fired on us and saying loudly: "You Hutus, come back here! The Tutsis killed our president so they must be killed too!" Mum asked me if I had followed well the scene. I replied that it was very terrible; Mum took the money for my school fees (5500 Francs, almost equivalent to 25 USD at that time) and handed it to me.

She told me that as my sister-in-law is not Tutsi, I could take the money and go with her, watch my two younger brothers and go to Rwamagana town through her village: "Do not say to any person that you are Tutsi or that you are escaping," she told me. We led the way with my two younger brothers John Ndagijimana and Emmanuel Bizimana (all alive) and my sister-in-law. It was 20 kilometres from Rwamagana. It was in the holidays of Esther.

At Rwamagana Town

At Rwamagana, there were my brother, my paternal aunt with three children, and my paternal uncle with his family. When I reached there all those were alive. They were very happy because there were some bad news which stated that we were all killed. After an hour or two, Dad, elder brother, and young brother arrived. We met and thanked God that we were not killed all that time, but Mum with younger brother, other relatives, and many neighbors left

there (at that hill) while the killers were killing
people on that hill.

Rwamagana Exile

Before we reached Rwamagana where those relatives
were, we reached the sister-in-law's place without any
problem, but on our way all the people were troubled
in general and every person had his own thoughts, but
there was no solution at all. The three brothers of my
sister-in-law saw us, and they called their sister and
asked how could she come with the enemies in their
houses. That time all Tutsis were called snakes and to
kill a snake it is very good because in society everybody fears a snake. I felt more fearful after she told me
aforesaid ideas.

We went to bed but we could not sleep at all. In the
morning of the following day, I suggested to my
sister-in-law that I knew well the way to my brother's
where I had a lot of relatives. First I had to see how
the situation is, I could hurry up and come back to
collect my younger brother. She accepted my suggestion but she argued: "Do not think that this place is
safe!" She wanted me to understand that her brothers
will kill my brothers. "So, hurry up and come back,
collect your brothers with you," she added. I went
quickly because I knew well the way. I could not lead
the main road because there were barriers everywhere, but I reached my brother's home without any
problem and I told him about what happened to us. I

immediately told him that I had to return back to see
our younger brothers at our sister-in-law's. I returned
there and when I reached there my younger brothers
had been crying because they listened to the conversation among our sister-in-law, her mother, and her
brothers, [who] were saying that they could kill the
enemies (snakes). I took them and farewelled my
sister-in-law and we went to Rwamagana town. It was
almost 5 kilometres from Rwamagana. We took small
ways. After 15 minutes we realized that we were
among the Interahamwe (almost 300 people). We
whispered, "This is our last time." They had all rudi-
mentary weapons (machetes, spears). They ordered us
to sit down and answer their questions. After few
minutes, they determined to kill us, but one young
man who was my classmate came saw me sitting down
among the Interahamwe and he asked me: "Isaie,
what's wrong?" I did not answer him because of fear.
He told the Interahamwe that he knew me very well,
so they had to let me go because I was not snake
(Tutsi), according to his explanation. After a long discussion with Interahamwe, they concluded to let us go.

He explained me which way to take in order to
reach my brother's home without any other problem.
We reached there safely. This, my classmate, is called
Innocent Tegibanze, may God bless him.

The situation in Rwamagana town was almost
safer, because we spent three days there and no
person was killed, except plundering some shops and

there were some barriers on the road. Three days later, the situation was worsened because the killers began killing Tutsis, but it was too late for them because the RPF soldiers were about to reach Rwamagana town (7 kilometres).

Interahamwe (Killers) Are Defeated
Between the 16th and 18th of April, the goverment police and the army patrolled and controlled everything, said to people: "The RPF soldiers are killing all people, whether you are Tutsi or Hutu." They mobilized all people to leave Rwamagana. It was a plan to call all Tutsis where they were hiding and kill them. The army and the police defeated and called all people to go to Zaza (another village far from Rwamagana). All people (Hutus and Tutsis) with the army and the police led the way to Zaza. The Tutsis who were with them were killed after reaching Zaza village. Among those who were killed, there were: my aunt with three children, my uncle with his son, and many other relatives of mine.

The RPF soldiers reached Rwamagana where we were hid early in the morning. I was the first to see them and recognized them beacause they were different from the government army, they had guns different from the government army's. I went with them after some questionings in order to show them where I expected people hid. After that, we were gathered in one camp at Kayonza town at 15 kilometres from

Rwamagana. Truly speaking, it was for us a good occasion even if a lot of Tutsis were killed, but we could not expect that there were still survivors.

After Genocide

The Rwandan government of Unity and Reconciliation was established on July 4th, 1994. It was very terrible throughout the country; there were a lot orphans, widows and widowers, trauma, poverty; there were no houses because the killers had burnt all Tutsis' houses, there were much major problems in the country. For me, life had become boring. I was completely disappointed. First, when I knew that someone was Hutu, I could ask him how he killed people and were not killed, either. I was always very sad! I could not imagine, even any other person could not imagine, how a man could kill a pregnant woman—example of my elder sister who was killed while she was pregnant. In my village, there was one neighbor, an old woman of 80 years, she could not walk nor eat except drinking some milk. The killers had killed her too. All those facts and many others disturbed me.

In 1995, I went to school to complete my secondary studies. Before Genocide I was in senior five, and I had to start senior five over again. I studied one day, the other day I could drink so much beer until I could not walk. I thought that there was no need to live or to study because during the genocide, the killers were aiming at exterminating first anybody who had studied. Although I had behaved in such a way, I did all my best in the last month of study, and God helped me, I passed the examination of the secondary school and I got my Diploma.

In 1998, I met a missionary woman from England (whose name I do not remember). She taught us how we could understand what happened to us and she convinced me. From that time, my obstacles in life sensibly reduced. I had a good job and I planned and got married on September 8th, 2001. One step after another, I was becoming happier and happier, and I was struggling to love everybody. In 2005, I got a job in Intercontinental Hotel Kigali after almost one year with no job. It is there that I met [the woman] whom I have the right to call "Mum" and I learned from her how people can love each other and what is a dignified man. From that time, I grew happier than ever with my family (my beloved wife, Clarisse, and my son, David), with my neighbors, and with everybody, especially the children. I am now filled with forgiveness even for those who were killers. I have now a vision and a good will in me of looking afar and succeeding in all of my projects. I have started my courses at the University, in the Faculty of Economics in "Université Libre de Kigali" and my studies are going well. All [this] it is from Mum. "May God bless her so much." *I would like that the whole world understands and supports the survivors of the Rwandan Genocide of 1994.*

All of us, young and old, have to follow Mum's way for making the world live in harmony by loving our fellow people. Living in harmony cannot be compared to anything else. People should be united in order to live in harmonious world. Such a life could be restored if people wished to do so. Reconciliation and peace can lead to a true harmony.

I leave the reader with this testimony that debunks the myth about the involvement of only a few in the population—that it was mainly military, paramilitary groups, and police who did most of the killing. In this eyewitness account you will find not only all the characters in this genocidal tragedy; embedded in this story are the ways and means of bullying, the breakdown of moral inhibitions, the pleasure from inflicting pain, the unquestioning obedience to authority, the routinization of cruelty, and the dehumanization of those targeted. This, in the account of Menachem Finkelsztajn, is what happened in the small town of Radzilow, Poland, on June 22, 1941:

The attitude of the peasants toward the Jews was very bad.... Poles from the vicinity ridiculed frightened Jews and, motioning across their necks, kept saying, "Now it will be cut up *Jude*" [*Teraz bedzie rznij Jude*]. The Polish population immediately cozied up to the Germans. They built a triumphal arch to greet the German army decorated with a swastika, a portrait of Hitler, and a sign: "Long live the German army, which liberated us from the horrible grip of the Judeo-commune!"... Germans beat Jews mercilessly and robbed them of their property and then distributed the stolen items among the Poles ... took their cows away and gave them to the Poles.... On the 24th, soldiers ordered the Jews to bring out all the holy books and Torahs from the synagogue and the prayer house and burn them. When the Jews refused, Germans ordered them to unroll the Torahs and to douse them with kerosene, and they set them alight. They ordered Jews to sing and dance around the huge burning pile. Around the dancing Jews a jeering crowd was assembled that beat them freely. When the holy books burned down, they harnessed Jews to carts and ordered them to pull while beating them mercilessly.... Screams of pain were frequently piercing the air. But together with these screams one could hear happily screaming Polish and German sadists who were sitting in the carts. Poles and Germans continued to torment the Jews until they chased them to a swampy little river near the town. Jews were ordered there to undress completely and to get up to their necks in the swamp. Sick and old men, who could not obey these beastly orders, were beaten up and thrown into even deeper swamps....

And so on the 26th of June, on Friday evening, they (Poles) sent a group of German soldiers to our house. Like wild animals the tormentors dispersed around the house searching and throwing around everything they found ... foodstuffs they also threw out and doused with kerosene ... when they finished destroying things, they started beating my father....

One could feel it; it was in the air, that the Polish population was getting ready for a pogrom. That's why we all decided that my mother should go and plead with the local priest, Aleksander Dolegowski, whom we knew well. We wanted him, as a spiritual leader of the community, to influence the believers not to take part in the persecution of the Jews. But how great was our disappointment when the priest, with anger, replied, "It is well known that every Jew, from the youngest to those sixty years old, are communists," and said that he had no interest whatsoever in defending them. My mother tried to argue that his position was false, that even if someone deserved to be punished, women and small children were surely innocent? She appealed to his conscience to have pity and stop a dark mob that was ready to commit all kinds of atrocities that in the future would certainly stand as a shame to the Polish nation, because the political situation would not always remain as it was then. But his cruel heart did not soften, and he said in the end that he could not say anything good about the Jews, because his believers would throw mud on him. The same answer was received from all the other prominent Christian town citizens to whom the Jews appealed to intervene in this matter.

The consequences of these refusals were not long in coming. On the very next day squads of young

Polish sons were organized ... who inflicted terrible moral and physical pain on the frightened and miserable Jews. From morning till night they led the old Jews, laden with sacred books, to a nearby river. They were sent on their march by crowds of Christian women, children, and men. When they got to the river, the Jews had to throw their books into the water. They also had to lie down, get up, hide their heads, swim, and perform other idiotic exercises. Spectators laughed loudly and applauded. Murderers stood over their victims and beat them mercilessly if they didn't execute an order. They also took women and girls and ordered them to get wet in the river.

On the way back squads armed with sticks and iron bars surrounded the tired, barely alive Jews and gave them a beating. And when one of the tortured protested, refused to obey orders, and threatened and cursed them, saying that they would be taken to account for this soon, they beat him so that he lost consciousness. After nightfall squads assaulted Jews in their houses, by breaking down windows and doors. They took the hated Jews out, beat them till the Jews fell down bloodied and unconscious. Not even women and children, or mothers with newborn babies, were spared. From time to time they brought Jews from their houses to the square and they beat them there. The screams were unbearable. Around the tortured ones crowds of Polish men, women, and children were standing and laughing at the miserable victims who were falling under the blows of the bandits. There were many wounded and mortally sick Jews as a result of these orgies. And their number was increasing day by day. The only Polish doctor who was in town, Jan Mazurek, refused medical assistance to people who had been beaten.

The situation was worsening day by day. The Jewish population became a toy in the hands of the Poles. There were no German authorities as the army moved on and did not leave power to anyone.

The only one who had influence and maintained some sort of order was the priest, who mediated between Christians in their affairs. It was not simply that the Jews were of no concern to anybody; propaganda started coming out from the upper echelons of Polish society which influenced the mob, stating that it was time to settle scores with those who had crucified Jesus Christ, with those who take Christian blood for matzoh and are a source of all evil in the world—the Jews. Let's stop playing around with the Jews. It is time to cleanse Poland of these pests and bloodsuckers. The seed of hatred fell on well-nourished soil, which had been prepared for many years by the clergy.

The wild and bloodthirsty mob took it as a holy challenge that history had put upon it—to get rid of the Jews. And the desire to take over Jewish riches whetted their appetites even more....

Who killed them (a man and his young daughter)? Polish murderers ... who had been raised for decades by a reactionary clergy, who bolstered their existence by preaching racial hatred....

To the newly established Polish municipal authorities made up of a priest, the doctor, a former secretary of the *gmina* Stanislaw Grzymkowski, and a few other prominent Poles a delegation was sent to plead with them to stop what the population was doing. They replied that they could not help and sent the Jews to people from the underworld, to negotiate with them. Those in turn said that the Jews should compensate them, and then everybody's lives would be spared. Jews, thinking that this might be their last chance, started bringing to Wolf Szlepen [?] various valuables; china, suits, sewing machines [?], gifts of silver and gold; they also promised to give up cows that they had hidden. But all this was a comedy organized by murderers. The fate of Radzilow's Jews was already sealed. As was later learned, the Polish population knew one day ahead when the Jews would be liquidated and in what manner.... What a terrible sight this presented can be gauged from the fact that the Germans stated that the Poles had gone overboard. The arrival of the Germans saved eighteen Jews who had managed to hide during the pogrom. There was an eight-year-old boy among them, who had already been buried, but who revived and dug himself out.... In this manner the Jewish community in Radzilow was wiped off the face of the earth after five hundred years of existence. Together with the Jews everything Jewish was destroyed in the village as well: the study house, the synagogue, and the cemetery.

Several pages are missing from Finkelsztajn's testimony, but in a testimony published in the memorial book of Grajewo Jews, it is documented that, in the end, Radzilow Jews, "sixty multigenerational families including, children, parents, and grandparents," were assembled in the square, where many were beaten and some murdered. Those still alive were then brought to the Mitkowski barn and burned.

The voice of conscience and humanity will never be silenced in me, and therefore I address these words to you.... This document is a testament. It is the tongues of a thousand dead that I speak in it.... If you, Mr. President, have indeed made the sublime idea of championing oppressed nations the guiding principle of your policy, you will not fail to perceive that even in these words a mighty voice speaks, the only voice that has the right to be heard at all times— the voice of humanity.

—ARMIN T. WEGNER, AN EYEWITNESS
TO GENOCIDE, IN AN OPEN LETTER
TO PRESIDENT WILSON, JANUARY 1919

Beware the Wolf in Sheep's Clothing

Germany is nothing. Each individual German is everything.

—GOETHE, 1808

The power of choosing between good and evil is
within the reach of all.

—ORIGEN (C. 185–254)

Just as it is possible for one person to play several roles in
the tragedy of genocide, it is also possible that, on the
stage, looks can be deceiving. For example, a person
dressed as a physician—someone who has taken an oath
to save lives—can be a planner, instigator, perpetrator,
henchman, active supporter, passive supporter, disengaged onlooker, potential witness, witness-defender-
resister, or target. And the same is true in the case of
other professions, such as civil servants, lawyers, human
rights activists, teachers, scientists, and religious leaders.
When those who have professed to be "helpers" or
"healers" in a society violate that promise, or, in the case
of the medical community, their oath, part of the healing
and restoration that must take place after a genocide is
the rebuilding of the trust in and integrity of that profession. It is also those in these professions who are highly
prized targets, because they are often leaders in their
communities. So it is a double blow to a post-genocide
society to try to restructure a functioning community
when people in those professions are in short supply
because they are exiled, dead, mutilated, devastated, or
imprisoned.

The following are examples of the various roles in a
genocide played by people in the medical community.

WITNESS AND DEFENDER

In his memoirs, Samuel H. Zorian tells of the kindness of the doctor who visited him in prison after he was arrested by the Turkish government as intellectuals and prominent Armenians were being rounded up for deportation or death:

> The city authority's doctor, Dr. Chboukdjyan from Constantinople, and his pharmacist assistant, Hakob *effendi*, visited the prison once a week. With impatience and eagerness I greeted those occasions, for the kind and cultured doctor not only treated me with compassion but, after examining me, promised to send me some good medicine. In spite of the presence of the prison warder, he always spoke to me in Armenian, and above all he would never leave without giving me a smile.

PLANNER, INSTIGATOR, AND PERPETRATOR

In the spirit of *Gleichschaltung* (marching in step), Hitler pressed into the service of the regime professionals in the fields of education, technology, media, science, and medicine to influence public opinion and perception. Doctors not only colluded with the regime, they took the lead in promoting racist policies and outnumbered other professionals in embracing the Nazi Party and filling its ranks. One of the most notorious was Josef Mengele, the second son of a well-to-do, devout Catholic family. He put his intellectual gifts, his medical skills, his fascination with heredity research, his material wealth, and his religious fervor to diabolical use in Auschwitz. He personally selected prisoners on the railway ramp as they arrived into the camp, sorting them out according to "those saved and those damned"—all to be damned, ultimately, either through instant death in the gas chambers or slow death through Mengele's grisly genetics and germ experiments. In one of his projects he infected identical and fraternal Jewish and Roma twins with typhoid bacteria, then analyzed their blood as disease took hold, until the death of the twins, never once using his medical skills to alleviate their suffering.

The horrors inflicted by the medical community during the genocide warranted a new term to characterize the intentional mutilations, experimentations, and killings done by professionals supposedly dedicated to saving lives. One of the prosecutors at the Nürnberg trials, Telford Taylor, chose *thanatology*, the science of death, to describe the charges laid against the doctors.

TARGET

In his book *Hitler's Scientists: Science, War, and the Devil's Pact*, John Cornwell writes of one Jewish doctor's story that "provides a moving impression of the everyday predicament" of those Jewish doctors who lived in Germany under Hitler. Doctor Hertha Nathorff, a gynecologist married to a senior Jewish hospital doctor, detailed in her diary the way the government worked to exclude, isolate, and eventually remove Jewish doctors from Germany, beginning in 1933. As anti-Semitic remarks from clinic patients escalated, Jewish surgeons were barred from operating theaters and doctors turned away from their hospitals. Dr. Nathorff's husband was fired by his hospital and began a private practice:

> Jewish doctors were put on the back of open trucks and paraded around the streets while pedestrians jeered.... In May a patient broke down and wept ... the woman had been at the point of gassing herself because she believed that, since she once had sexual relations with a Jew, she would not be able to conceive a pure Aryan child.... One of her patients, unaware that Nathorff was Jewish, told her "everything will be fine when all the filthy Jews have been thrown out of Germany"...
>
> The oppression continued unabated ... her midwife assistant ... had been advised that she should join the Reich Midwife Association, which precluded her working any longer for a Jew. A patient came to say that she could no longer come to consultation because her teenage sons had threatened to denounce her ... a patient came asking for poison to end her life; after discovering she had a Jewish grandmother, she had lost her job and her boyfriend.

Dr. Nathorff's physician husband was briefly arrested on *Kristallnacht*, Night of the Broken Glass, as he worked all night to treat the injured, traumatized, and ill. With a gun held to her head in front of her young son, Hertha handed over a large sum of money to get her husband released. They finally were allowed to flee to New York, but by law were required to leave all valuables, silver cutlery, jewelry, and property, taking only the barest essentials and a small sum of money for their journey.

PLANNER, INSTIGATOR, AND PERPETRATOR

In Rwanda, as in the other two genocides, doctors violated the basic ethical code of their profession. There were doctors who were senior members of the government, and others who actively participated in the murders, at times killing their own colleagues and patients. Two doctors were senior members of the interim government. Pediatrician Théodore Sindikubwabo was president. Formerly an intelligence officer of the MRND party (Mouvement Révolutionnaire National pour le Développement), the Minister of Health, Dr. Casimir Bizimungu, incited ethnic hatred with his writings in the extremist journal *Kangura*. Other doctors expelled Tutsi patients to face a certain death. Dr. Jeanne Nduwamariya was regarded by many as one of the "most fanatical extremists" in Butare, chiding the Interahamwe for their failure to kill women on her own personal hit list.

> There must have been a moment at the beginning, where we all could have said no. But somehow we missed it.
>
> —TOM STOPPARD, *ROSENCRANTZ AND GUILDENSTERN ARE DEAD*

THE ROLE OF RELIGION— SCRIPTED AND UNSCRIPTED

We stand with you ... in your proclamation of
"Never Again" should genocide unfold anywhere
else, but also never again should religious leaders
choose to be on the wrong side of peace.

—PRESIDENT PAUL KAGAME, SPEAKING AT THE
OFFICIAL LAUNCH OF THE INTERFAITH ACTION
FOR PEACE IN AFRICA (IFAPA), JUNE 19, 2006

The failure of the leadership of the religious communities to
speak out during the genocide of the Tutsis—and for some
in the highest ranks to actively participate in planning, instigating, and perpetrating the mass extermination of the
Tutsis—rendered the hierarchies of all the major churches
morally and spiritually bankrupt. And until these leaders'
acts of omission and commission are scrutinized and individuals and institutions held to account, the churches and their
leaders will continue "to choose to be on the wrong side of
peace." The human rights organization African Rights has
documented the actions of many nuns and priests who stood
up for those who were targeted and courageously defied the
genocidaires. These deeds perhaps succeeded in convincing
the people of Rwanda "that Christian values of solidarity,
truth and love do still exist," even though they were
painfully absent in the institution and hierarchy of the
churches. During my trips to Rwanda I saw and heard
stories about members of the various religious communities
who assumed the roles of *genocidaires*, bystanders, defenders,

resisters, witnesses, and targets. The same can be said of the two other genocides studied in this book.

It was with a heavy heart and troubled mind that I, a former Franciscan nun, studied the complicity of religion in these genocides. Such complicity was omitted from the history books I studied in high school and barely touched upon in university texts—and even the commentary that did exist was often one-sided and biased. In this brief history, I make no pretense to even touch upon all the ways in which religion has been used by the *genocidaires* to reinforce what anthropologist and social scientist Dr. John Hartung describes as "in-group morality" and "out-group hostility" to justify cruelty and to rally the masses to do their bidding in excluding, tormenting, and exterminating these outsiders.

The Ottoman Turks wanted to rid their empire of the Armenians who were the Christian minority—the Infidels. In the beginning of that genocide, one way to avoid deportation, starvation, or extermination was to convert to Islam, willingly or by force—by fire and sword.

The Nazis followed the Christian tradition of seeing Jews as the evil "other," the "Christ-killers." They accused Jews of "blood libel"—killing non-Jews in order to get their blood for use in religious rituals. Forced conversions through baptism and kidnapping of Jewish children "to save their souls" was practiced in many places in Europe, even before the rise of Nazism. Martin Luther espoused a rabid anti-Semitism, calling Jews a "brood of vipers." Cries of *"Hep!"* (*"Hierosolyma est perdita,"* "Jerusalem is destroyed") could be heard in the streets of Nazi Germany during the pogroms that preceded the genocide of the Jews. Through silence, and acts of omission as well as commission, both the Protestant and Catholic Churches have sordid records of complicity with the Nazis.

Born into a Catholic family, attending Catholic schools and church regularly, Hitler took to heart a moral absolutism and strict obedience to authority. In a speech in 1923, he described it as his Christian duty to rid the world of Jews: "The first thing to do is rescue [Germany] from the Jew who is ruining our country.... We want to prevent Germany from suffering, as Another did, the death upon the Cross." After 1941, Hitler appeared to do an about-face, espousing virulent anti-Christian views.

Tutsis fled to the churches in search of safe harbor, only to have the *genocidaires* mock them as they hacked them to death among the pews, on the altars, and in baptismal fonts, chanting, "Even God has forsaken you; even He won't save a cockroach."

For many of the individuals who did speak out, reached out, or risked their lives to rescue others during the genocide of the Armenians in 1915, the genocide of Jews, Roma, and Sinti in World War II, the genocide of the Tutsis in 1994, and the genocide in Darfur, religion played a minor role, if any, in their decision to act. Many saw what they did as a *must*, but not because they felt bound by religious tenets. In fact, many had no professed religion and some acted in direct opposition to their church leaders and church dogma.

The distinguished Holocaust historian Raul Hilberg wrote, "There are some things that can be done so long as they are not discussed, for once they are discussed, they can no longer be done." There must be a healthy debate about the good, the bad, the ugly, and the indifferent inherent in religious traditions, religious taboos, and religious hatreds. It is time for a discussion in our homes, our schools, and our communities—and as a world community—about the complicity of religion in hate crimes and crimes against humanity, about indifference, about apathy, and about how *genocidaires* use religion as a pretext to turn morality on its head. We need to explore the dangers of the "them versus us" scenario that, bound up in religious terms, becomes a cataclysmic battle between good and evil. We must examine sentiments that condone intolerance and violence. And we must become very concerned when religion and state become bound up as one, when religion and nationalism join forces. Some in Nazi Germany went one step further, turning Nazism into a state religion. A salute written by a senior officer in a German trade union at this time offers adulation of Hitler and thanks to Providence for this leader.

Adolf Hitler! We are united with you alone! We want to renew our vow in this hour: On this earth we believe only in Adolf Hitler. We believe that National Socialism is the sole saving faith for our people. We believe that there is a Lord God in heaven, who created us, who leads us, who directs us and who blesses us visibly. And we believe that this Lord God sent Adolf Hitler to us, so that Germany might become a foundation for all eternity.

I have come to the realization that religion is neither sufficient nor necessary in order for someone to act with integrity, civility, and compassion, to stand up and speak out against injustice, to do the right thing simply because it's the right thing to do. When asked about his beliefs, the renowned war photographer James Natchwey answered, "I do not put my faith in God or divine intervention. I put my hope in humanity because all we have is each other." Natchwey, who has witnessed some of the most horrific acts of violence committed against children and photographed the mayhem in hopes of shattering our collective indifference to the horrors of war, mass murder, and genocide, still puts his hope in humanity. Can those of us who have witnessed far less not do the same?

Natchwey's hope for humanity is bound up in a relationship of caring. This relationship is premised on what philosopher Martin Buber called "meeting one another as an I and a Thou." To see another as a "Thou" is to honor our uniqueness and our individuality, and at the same time to recognize our common bond, our solidarity and interdependence. What seems a paradox is actually two necessary parts of the whole: our individuality and our commonality. We are both an "I and a Thou" and a "We." When we dehumanize another, making them into an "It," we destroy the "Thou," diminish ourselves, and destroy our common bond. Each one of us depends on the well-being of the whole; if our common bond is destroyed, each one of us is less.

Religion has the potential to either destroy that bond or to strengthen it.

Religion can be harmful inasmuch as it serves to divide us. Inasmuch as it serves to give some people a sense of entitlement, a liberty to exclude, and intolerance toward differences. Inasmuch as it denies equal rights and partnership between men and women. Inasmuch as it fails to support a just economic order and basic human rights. Intolerance, bigotry, and hatred wrapped in the garb of religion are still intolerance, bigotry, and hatred.

Religion can be helpful inasmuch as it helps us to honor the "I and Thou" and the "We." Inasmuch as it validates the intrinsic dignity of each human being and affirms our solidarity and our interdependence. Inasmuch as it provides rituals and ethical traditions that help us develop our authentic selves in relation to a genuine community.

Religion can be a source of good inasmuch as it helps us to develop an ethic rooted not in principles, rules, customs, or dogma, but in deep caring—caring deeply for our own children and our neighbors and their children, and nurturing their innate ability to care, helping them to see themselves as both lovable and loving.

Can we wish others abundant joy and a quiet peace? Can we show a deep passion to alleviate another's pain and sorrow and let that become a part of our everyday life? Can we reach out to others who are suffering their own personal tragedies and ask, "What are you going through?" "What do you need?" "What can I do?" Can we be there for them as they name their loss, honor their grief, confront their pain, and tell their story? Can we also rejoice in their joys, their accomplishments, and their gains? Can we wish them enough as we take only what we need? This is the human wisdom that enables us to meet one another morally—regardless of our belief or nonbelief.

I think we can't go around measuring our goodness
by what we don't do, by what we deny ourselves,
what we resist, and who we exclude. I think we've got
to measure goodness by what we embrace, what we
create, and who we include.
                    —PÈRE HENRI, IN THE FILM *CHOCOLAT*

If people are good only because they fear punishment, and hope for reward, then we are a sorry lot
indeed.
                                        —ALBERT EINSTEIN

Chapter 6

Scenes from a Tragedy

We worry that explaining Evil condones it.
We have to maintain our outrage at Hitler. But
wouldn't it be nice to have a theory of evil in
advance that could keep him from coming to
power…? A system a bit more focused on helping
people change rather than paying them back for
what they've done might be a good thing.

—DAN WEGNER

Bully, bullied, and *bystander* are terms that identify only
roles played at a particular moment, in just one scene of one
act in a longer play. They do not necessarily define or
permanently label the people playing those roles. In fact,
once the curtain closes on the tragedy of genocide, many
instigators, perpetrators, and accomplices go on to lead
"respectable" lives in their communities, most often never
called to account for their actions during the genocide,
rationalizing their roles as actually fulfilling a civic duty of
ridding their communities of the enemy.

The goal of labeling and examining these roles is to gain
a better understanding of them, and to see more clearly

how the interactions involved in such role-playing are not healthy, not normal, and certainly not necessary—are, in fact, devastating to the whole of society. Recognizing, labeling, and examining these roles is step one in rewriting the script that leads to genocide. Step two is analyzing the scenes that are played out in the tragedy itself.

SETTING THE SCENE FOR GENOCIDE

- An environment is created that nurtures and facilitates in homes, schools, and the community unquestioning obedience to authority, the routinization of cruelty, and the dehumanization of a people.
- The atmosphere is infused with hate—especially the cold hate of contempt. (Hate destroys the "Thou," rendering the other an "It.")
- These are coupled with hoarding, with its rapacious and exploitive individualism that blinds us to the needs of others and their rightful place in a genuine community.
- Added is the ability to harm—lie, cheat, and steal—with impunity, which in turn violates the critical bonds of trust.
- The media noise that fuels all of the above is cranked up.
- Diversionary conflict is staged to create a fog to hide the "gorilla in our midst."
- Thrown into the mix is an international community that turns a blind eye to the suffering and a deaf ear to the cries of those who are targeted.

ACT ONE: SURVEYING THE LANDSCAPE

The bullies survey the stage, check out the other characters in an attempt to identify potential targets, and look to the audience to see if anyone in the international community is paying attention.

The potential targets go about their daily lives, unaware or only vaguely aware that they are being stereotyped, prejudged, or discriminated against.

Bystanders blithely go about their daily lives, soaking up the stereotypes and prejudices, all the while enjoying the company and comradeship of one another, creating, without much thought, a deeply ingrained sense of "us and them."

ACT TWO: TEST RUN

Using crude and hurtful taunts, and hate propaganda to depersonalize the targeted group, the bullies verbally and relationally attack the targeted group and observe their reactions, as well as the reactions of the bystanders and the audience.

The bullied react with a shrug, slump down, are uneasy, feel fear in the gut, but don't know what to do.

The bystanders either look away or laugh, giving support and tacit approval to the bullies. For some this is a form of entertainment at the targets' expense.

ACT THREE: ACTION

Viewing their targets as objects of ridicule and scorn, not as equals, the bullies organize physical attacks on the bullied, their personal belongings, and their property.

The bullied feel powerless against the bullies, try to rationalize what is happening, may blame themselves for the attacks.

Some bystanders move away from the scene and feel guilty for not stopping the bullies. They may feel helpless and afraid themselves; some worry that they will be next. Other bystanders join in, verbally taunt the targets, and may join in the physical assaults. Others go in to collect the booty, take advantage of job openings, and lay claim to abandoned or seized property. The process of depersonalization and desensitization enables both the bullies and the bystanders to commit more severe acts of violence and aggression against the targeted group.

ACT FOUR: EMBOLDENED

The bullies find new opportunities to taunt, torment, physically harm, and isolate the targeted group—often using the legal system to confiscate goods, create ghettoes and/or concentration camps, validate the imposition of identity cards and identifying markings or symbols. The bullies become more physically aggressive and threaten more harm in order to instill terror in the targeted group. They feel powerful when engaging the targets. The terror created gives the bullies a sense of pleasure.

The bullied spend precious time figuring out ways to avoid the bullies, feel helpless and hopeless.

The bystanders again break into two camps: one group, feeling intimidated, steers clear of the bullies to avoid confrontation; the other group joins in the bullying. Both groups see the targeted group as being outside their limited circle of concern. Both groups fear—and the second may both fear and revere—the bullies and convince themselves that they won't be next by rationalizing that the targets had it coming, deserved what they got.

ACT FIVE: PINNACLE OF PAIN

The bullies continue to torment and hurt the targets with increasing viciousness. They become typecast in the role of bullies, fail to develop healthy relationships, lack the ability to take another's perspective, are void of empathy toward the targeted group, and view themselves as powerful and well liked. Their sense of entitlement, their intolerance, and their pleasure in excluding the targeted group from any human concern are the hallmarks of their reputation.

The bullied slump further into depression and/or rage—they are often angry with themselves, with the bullies, with the bystanders, and with the international community who wouldn't or couldn't help. Robbed of ways to make a living or maintain healthy relationships, they begin to resemble the dehumanized caricature the bullies portrayed them as.

Bystanders do one of four things: (1) remain fearful of the bullies and continue to blame the targets for becoming victims; (2) join the bullying; (3) not seeing anyone else intervening, convince themselves they are helpless to stop the bullying; or, worse yet, (4) see no need to stop it and move up the ranks of bystanders to become perpetrators or henchmen.

ACT SIX: FINALE

Bullies begin to "exterminate" with impunity the targeted group, making use of all the resources of the state. Occasionally they carry on a dialogue with the audience of the international community, justifying the need to eliminate a threat to the state. Or they may merely pretend that nothing out of the ordinary is going on. Sometimes the audience is invited to step onto the stage and, through acts of omission or commission, help the genocidal regime finish its task.

The bullied, not trusting the international community to protect or help them, do whatever it takes to get rid of their pain. Their pent-up rage may explode into violent aggression against the bullies and all those who appear to have helped them, those who stood by and did nothing, and those who failed to protect them. (The international community may wrongly place these reprisal killings into the category of bilateral genocide and judge the actions of the targeted group as morally equivalent to the genocidal actions of the bullies.)

Bystanders either get caught in the crossfire, feel guilt-ridden for not intervening, or become so desensitized to the violence that they minimize and normalize it and pass their assumption on to the next generation, at which point the stage is set for a reprise.

ENCORE

No sooner does the final curtain come down on this horrific tragedy than perpetrators and their accomplices begin the call for an encore—rarely in a flagrant call for the killings to begin anew, but rather through their persistent denial that the tragedy was a genocide. *Genocidaires* use any and all forms of excuse to contradict the reality.

DENIAL, APATHY, AND IMPUNITY

The massive trauma inflicted on the collective consciousness of the Armenian people is an open wound, continually aggravated by the refusal to acknowledge its infliction.... The future of the past remains uncertain.

—DONALD BLOXHAM, *THE GREAT GAME OF GENOCIDE*

In a paper presented at the Yale University Center for International and Area Studies in 1998, Gregory H. Stanton delineated eight stages of genocide: classification, symbolization, dehumanization, organization, polarization, preparation, extermination, and the last stage, denial. "[Denial] is among the surest indicators of further genocidal massacres. The perpetrators of genocide dig up the mass graves, burn the bodies, try to cover up the evidence and intimidate the witnesses. They deny that they committed any crimes, and often blame the victims. They block investigations of the crimes, and continue to govern until driven from power by force, when they flee into exile."

In his book *The Emergence of Modern Turkey*, Bernard Lewis writes that the massacres of the Armenians were the outcome of "a struggle between two nations for the possession of a single homeland," and that Talaat was "a man of swift and penetrating intelligence, forceful when necessary, but never fanatical or vengeful." The genocide "resulted from a more or less legitimate and just war between two more or less evenly matched adversaries." In a vain attempt to deny the genocide of the Armenians, Justin McCarthy, a professor of history at the University of Louisville in Kentucky, said, "The majority of those who were deported survived, even though those Armenians were completely at the mercy of the Ottomans. It was not genocide." In August 1994, the former prefect of greater Kigali, François Karera, made a similar claim: "You cannot use that word genocide because there are numerous [Tutsis] surviving." Lewis Brandon, the editor of *The Journal of Historical Review*, offered a helpful suggestion to those who maintain that the genocide of the Jews is a gigantic hoax, some kind of Zionist conspiracy: "If we are able to demonstrate effectively that six million Jews were not 'gassed' but were simply a product of the Zionists' Machiavellian imaginations ..."

On April 27, 1994, on the floor of the Knesset, Israel's foreign minister, Yossi Beilin, said, in response to a TV interview in which the Turkish ambassador had denied the genocide of the Armenians and called it "a war": "It was not war. It was most certainly massacre and genocide, something the world must remember.... We will always reject any attempt to erase its record, even for some political advantage." If only other countries would take such a politically unpopular but ethical stand. The stated position of the American government on the genocide of the Armenians was one of downright condemnation from 1916 through to April 8, 1975, when House Resolution 148 designated April 24, 1975, "'National Day of Remembrance of Man's Inhumanity to Man' ... for all the victims of genocide, especially the one and one-half million people of Armenian ancestry who succumbed to the genocide perpetrated in 1915." But only five years later, the State Department began referring instead to "the ambiguous facts of the massacres." Viewing Turkey as an important military partner, in 2005 the Bush administration refused to recognize two resolutions passed by congressional committee to call the mass slaughter of the Armenians a "genocide." Discussing the role of the United States in international affairs, including its possible intervention to stop a genocide, U.S. ambassador to the United Nations John Bolton said, without ambiguity or embarrassment: "The only question for the U.S. is what's our national interest, and if you don't like that, I'm sorry but that's the fact." Such a morally corrupt position— refusing to intervene when there is "only a humanitarian interest," not a national interest—is extremely short-sighted, narrow-minded, and cold-hearted.

On the genocide of the Armenians, the French took a far different stance, adopting a bill on January 18, 2001, stating that "France publicly recognizes the Armenian genocide of 1915." In December 2006 the French postal service released a stamp commemorating the genocide. However, when I tried to purchase the stamps in January 2007, I was told, "The stamps are no longer available." Could the protests in Paris have influenced the decision?

On April 21, 2004, the Canadian House of Commons passed a Bloc Québécois motion: "This House acknowledges the Armenian genocide of 1915 and condemns this act as a crime against humanity." After pressure from the Turkish government regarding a joint NATO exercise, the Canadian government decided to establish a committee to investigate "both sides of the story." Governments can bully not just their own people but other governments as well. And political interests far too often trump humanitarian interests.

The author of the comprehensive Arusha Report on the genocide in Rwanda, Gerry Caplan, identifies many of the international bystanders who saw it in their own "best interests" to deny the reality of the genocide of the Tutsis.

There are always deniers. There are always David Irvings and Ernst Zundels, who for their own sordid or pathological motives deny what can't be doubted. In Rwanda's case, it's an unholy coalition of Hutu *genocidaires* who want to complete the extermination of the Tutsi, whites in Belgium and France who had

privileged access to the pre-genocide Hutu government, conservative Christian politicians in Europe,
and a motley cast of characters around the world
(including Canadians) with diverse, perverse, sometimes inexplicable motives.

Caplan brings to the fore the international communities'
complex complicity in that genocide and invites us to
examine more closely such complicity in the other genocides. Knowingly providing financial aid or weapons, training and arming the *genocidaires'* armies and militias, make
bystanders complicit in the death of millions. But what is at
work here is not only what Martin Luther King, Jr., called
the "vitriolic actions of those who are bad," but also "the
vitiating inaction of those who are good." To stand by
rather than stand up, to turn away rather than come to the
aid of those who are targeted, or to refuse to get involved
because "it is not in our national interest" is to rend the
fabric of our humanity and tear apart our sense of community. These "vitriolic actions" and "vitiating inactions," the
denial, guilt, shame, indifference, and "us and not them" or
"us versus them" kind of cognitive dissonance that happens
to the world at large in the aftermath of genocide inevitably
sever our connections to one another.

If denial, apathy, and impunity are applauded, the
tragedy is repackaged and taken on the road to another
location, with a new cast of characters who have studied the
previous genocides and improved on the script. As I write
this book, the genocide in Darfur is not just beginning its

rehearsals, it is nearing its closing act. And in Iraq, the tragedy has already reached the Act Five "pinnacle of pain."

Since, as George H. Stanton stated, "[Denial] is among the surest indicators of further genocidal massacres," to prevent future genocides, it behooves us to first refuse to deny the reality of past genocides. Meeting sons and daughters of survivors of the genocide of the Armenians, their passion to have their parents' and grandparents' stories told was palpable. Deran Rushton-Zorian, translating his father's story, *This Man and Others, The Personal Memoirs of Samuel H. Zorian*, wrote the saying recited at the end of Armenian folk tales:

> *Veren idjav irek' khndsour,*
> *Meke indsi*
> *Meke hak'yat'e isoghin*
> *Mekelle Hafas khardjoghin.*

> Three apples fell from above
> One for me
> One for the teller of this tale
> And one for him who put his soul into it.

And he concluded with, "This is a popular saying in the Armenian dialect of Diyarbekir, with the difference that mine is not a folk tale but a fact." Genocide is fact, not myth or Machiavellian imagination.

In light of the vigorous attempts to deny the reality of the genocide of the Armenians, more and more people are

speaking up, risking censure, prison time, and for some—
such as the Turkish Armenian journalist Hrant Dink—
brutal murder, to make sure that the world does not forget.
It is far too easy and convenient to attempt to erase the past
and to rush on to form new strategic alliances, even with
those who perpetrated the genocides, with little or no
regard for the pain, suffering, and horrific losses experienced by those targeted for extermination. As the world
community rushes to move on from the last genocide, it
behooves us all to remember the words of Arnold J.
Toynbee: "When people proclaim that the past is not worth
remembering and present and future deserve to occupy all
our attention ... we can confidently look for a skeleton in
the cupboard."

> History is predominately the story of unlearned
> lessons.... If you deliberately ignore, think away,
> or deface the past, you are hampering yourself for
> taking intelligent action in the present.
> —ARNOLD J. TOYNBEE

Chapter 7

Restoring Community

Criminal prosecution after the fact doesn't
effectively prevent atrocity before the fact....
The atrocity trial, the legacy of Nürnberg, is *a*
means to justice and a modest one at that. It is
not *the* means to justice.

—PROFESSOR MARK DRUMBL,
NATIONAL PUBLIC RADIO, SEPTEMBER 28, 2006

The tragedy might be played out, the audience turn
their eyes away, the players move on to their next roles,
but the story does not end there. Those who have
survived face the daunting task of recreating their own
lives and reconstructing their communities. This includes,
but goes far beyond, the desire to bring the guilty to
justice.

Commenting on the Rwandan Tribunals, in which more
than one billion dollars was spent to issue major convictions for genocide, Professor Mark Drumbl suggested that
there was value to this investment, but perhaps some of
that money "could have gone elsewhere ... building
schools, compensating victims, creating jobs, and fighting

AIDS." In the aftermath of genocide, planners, instigators, and perpetrators must be brought to justice, but there are limits to the imposition of legal remedies.

Not all participants can realistically be imprisoned—the numbers are too large. But those who are not formally prosecuted can still be held to account. In Rwanda, various forms of restorative justice, including a modified form of an ancient healing circle, Gacaca, are being tried, with varying levels of success. Twelve years after the genocide of the Tutsis, Isaie Munyaneza participated in a Gacaca where some of the people responsible for the deaths of his family members were tried and convicted. For him it was part—but only a part—of his own healing. Others cannot bear to face those who tortured them or their families, especially when the *genocidaires* show no remorse or insist that they were only doing their "civic duty."

Truth-telling—the practice of telling all one knows about any and all killings one might have participated in, witnessed, or known about—has exposed some who would never have come forth on their own and exposed many of those who tried and failed to make sure all witnesses were killed. But there must be more than atrocity trials, Gacacas, and truth-telling to rebuild families, communities, countries—and in fact the world community—devastated by genocide. In *No Future Without Forgiveness*, Archbishop Desmond Tutu writes about the impact on all parties involved in the horrors of apartheid. His words are no less true for the horrors of genocide:

In one way or another, as a supporter, as a perpetrator, as a victim, or as one who opposed the ghastly system, something happened to our humanity. All of us ... were less whole.... Those who were privileged lost out as they became more uncaring, less compassionate, less humane, and therefore, less human.... Our humanity is caught up in that of all others. We are human because we belong. We are made for community, for togetherness, for family, to exist in a delicate network of interdependence.... We are sisters and brothers of one another whether we like it or not, and each one of us is a precious individual.

In the aftermath of genocide all of us are less whole. Beyond the legal remedies there must be reparations made to survivors, and the community must be healed through economic, social, cultural, and education programs that promote, at the minimum, coexistence—a coexistence in which people come together to build a strong community that is in the best interests, economically and socially, of each member. This "mutual self-interest" can then begin to create the "delicate network of interdependence" that works to counteract the "us and them" and "I and it" mindsets that lay the groundwork for the virulent contempt that fuels genocide.

Too often these monumental tasks—and those of tracking surviving relatives, finding bodies for proper burial, supporting orphans, creating remembrance rituals, and adequately treating all sorts of physical, mental, and emotional trauma—have been overlooked, minimized, or trivialized in the rush to get survivors to "forgive and move on," as if this would magically make whole that which was rent.

A QUESTION OF FORGIVENESS

> The survivor cannot stop himself from permanently going back to the genocide.... Even though a survivor may show pleasure in resuming his activities and take a fellow or a neighboring woman by the hand so as to hurry them up, he knows deep down that he is deluding himself. Even more so for he who speaks nothing but forgiving and forgetting and reconciliation.
>
> —JEAN-BAPTISTE MUNYANKORE,
> A SIXTY-YEAR-OLD TEACHER

In 1922, Ernst Werner Techow, a German right-wing terrorist, along with two others, assassinated Germany's Jewish Foreign Minister, Walther Rathenau, motivated by both political extremism and anti-Semitism. Mathilde Rathenau, the mother of the murdered man, wrote to Techow's mother:

> In grief unspeakable, I give you my hand—you of all women the most pitiable. Say to your son that, in the name of the spirit of him he has murdered, I forgive, even as God may forgive, if before an earthly judge your son makes a full and frank confession of his guilt ... and before a heavenly judge repents. Had he

known my son, the noblest man earth bore, he would have rather turned the weapon on himself. May these words give peace to your soul.

Techow was sent to prison but released for good behavior after five years. At the time of France's surrender to Nazi Germany, in 1940, Techow decided to smuggle himself into Marseilles, where he was able to help more than seven hundred Jews, rich and poor, escape to Spain with Moroccan permits.

Shortly before his activities in Marseilles, Techow met a nephew of Rathenau, and confided that his repentance and transformation had been triggered by Mathilde Rathenau's letter: "Just as Frau Rathenau conquered herself when she wrote that letter of pardon, I have tried to master myself. I only wished I would get an opportunity to right the wrong I have done."

Techow knew that no matter how many Jews he saved it would not alter the reality that Rabbi Walther Rathenau was dead, that murder "cannot be undone nor pardoned."

Jean-Baptiste, a convicted perpetrator in the genocide in Rwanda, also knows that he will have to live with the awful reality of his acts against the Tutsis: "There is now a crack in my life. I don't know about the others. I don't know if it is because of my Tutsi wife. But I know that the clemency of justice or the compassion of the stricken families can never fix this crack. Even the resurrection of the victims might not fix it. Perhaps not even my death will fix it."

Ahabaye inkovu hadasubirana. (A wound does not heal completely.)

—RWANDAN PROVERB

THE KILLERS

Bernadette Kabango wrote a poem to express her sorrow and grief, and how she untied the chains that bound her to those who had murdered her family members in the Rwandan genocide.

The Killers

The killers
You've invaded my nights
Singing your haunting lullaby
Drowning other voices
Choking, Suffocating, Numbing
Sending me to sleep

You've awakened me many mornings
Like an unexpected alarm
Shattering my dreams
Confusing, Terrorizing, Traumatizing
I've talked to you in tears and anger
Spat on you in rage
Whispered to you in sorrow
Tied you in chains
Thrown you in jail

I've pulled you out
Asked you many questions
Knowing there would be no answers ...

I tied you in chains
Again and again, round and round
Until the chains, in my dizziness
Bound me to you
You and I becoming one!
Bound by the chains of hate
I knew then the choices to make ...

I untied the chains
Letting go
Of those who converged on my dad
Beating, Pounding, Leaving him dead

I untied the chains
Letting go
Of those who propelled the grenade
Scattering my brother's brains

I untied the chains letting go
Of those who strangled
my sisters newly born
Leaving us a nameless grave

I untied the chains
Letting go

Of those who knifed my sister's throat
Leaving her begging for a better death

I untied the chains
Painfully, Purposefully
Knowing the one who said to do it
Seventy times seven
Totally understands the depth of my pain ...

On December 8, 2006, at a fundraiser in London, Ontario, for the Stephen Lewis Foundation, Bernadette sang this haunting song, accompanied by her son on guitar, as pictures of the genocide of the Tutsis flowed into one another in the background. The audience of three thousand Canadians, Africans, and Americans witnessed the passion and pain belonging only to one who knows firsthand of these chains.

POSSIBILITIES AND LIMITS OF FORGIVENESS

We who suffered in those dreadful days, we who cannot obliterate the hell we endured, are forever being advised to keep silent.
— SIMON WIESENTHAL, *THE SUNFLOWER: ON THE POSSIBILITIES AND LIMITS OF FORGIVENESS*

Simon Wiesenthal, imprisoned in a Nazi concentration camp, was taken one day from his work detail to the bedside of a young soldier. The Nazi soldier, a Catholic, felt haunted by his killing of Jews and had expressed a desire to confess to a Jew—any Jew would do—with the hope of obtaining forgiveness and absolution. The young Nazi needed to confess "in order to save his soul."

For hours the young man described the crimes in which he had participated, while Wiesenthal listened patiently. He even reached out and swatted a fly from the soldier's bandaged head. But when the soldier asked for his forgiveness in the name of all the Jews he had harmed or killed, Simon Wiesenthal walked silently out of the room.

After the war Wiesenthal went to work for the United States Army gathering evidence for the Nazi war crimes trials. Much of his life was dedicated to seeking information on and tracking down fugitive Nazis, so that they could be put on trial. He describes in his book *The Sunflower: On the Possibilities and Limits of Forgiveness* how the accused, when facing justice, were unlikely to show remorse and instead simply regretted that witnesses had survived to tell their stories. Wiesenthal asks the reader and himself, "Was my silence at the bedside of the dying Nazi wrong?" He imagines how the young soldier might have behaved if he had survived to be put on trial:

> Would he have spoken in the court as he did to me before he died in the Dean's room? Would he openly admit what he had confessed on his deathbed? Perhaps the picture that I formed of him in my mind was kinder than reality…. How could I have known if he would have committed further crimes had he survived?

Wiesenthal invites those reading the book to be challenged by the question he poses "just as much as it once challenged my heart and my mind. There are those who can appreciate my dilemma, and so endorse my attitude, and there are those who will be ready to condemn me for refusing to ease the last moment of a repentant murderer."

None of the perpetrators in these stories asked for forgiveness, except the young Nazi soldier, and none of those in a position to forgive, except Mathilde Rathenau (who forgave in the spirit of her son), mentioned forgiveness. Even Jean-Baptiste, a perpetrator, used the words "compassion of the stricken families."

And what about reconciliation? Mathilde Rathenau offered her son's murderer forgiveness, in her son's name, but she did not reconcile with him. Simon Wiesenthal remained silent and walked away. It raises the question: When horrific acts of violence are intentionally committed, are forgiveness and reconciliation necessary, or even good? What does forgiveness really mean? Is it a necessary part of reconciliation? Are the two even related and necessary to each other? Can you forgive and forget? Forgive and never forget? Can either be demanded? Is there an act that is beyond forgiveness?

WHAT'S FORGIVENESS GOT TO DO WITH IT?

I forgive, but I remember. I do not forget the pain,
the loneliness, the ache, the terrible injustice. But I

do not remember it to inflict guilt or some future
retribution. Having forgiven, I am liberated. I need
no longer be determined by the past. I move into the
future free to imagine new possibilities.

—LAWRENCE MARTIN JENCO, O.S.M.
BOUND TO FORGIVE

On January 8, 1985, Father Marty Jenco was kidnapped on
the streets of Beirut, Lebanon. He was held hostage until
July 16, 1986. His captivity was a journey through humiliation, deprivation, and torture, and for those of us who were
his friends it was a journey of chaos, loss, hope, and healing
for all. Marty and I spent many hours together discussing
the true meaning of forgiveness in light of what he had
endured, and survived.

The conclusion we came to is that forgiveness is not an
act of will. Forgiveness is the voice of the heart that speaks
in the presence of the soul. It is "heart business"—the mind
will be busy enough working out ways to demonstrate the
forgiveness: through feelings, deeds, actions, possibly
releasing debt, and making real other tangible expressions
of that forgiveness.

On being freed, Marty's response was, "I am liberated. I
need no longer be determined by the past. I move into the
future free to imagine new possibilities." His forgiveness
did not require that those who tortured him confess,
repent, or make restitution. That would again hold him
hostage to those who were intentionally cruel to him. In
fact, the forgiveness was not about them. It was an act of
"radical self-interest" in which he now had a sense that he

need not thirst for revenge or bear ill will against the men who had tortured him; his life from that point on would not be *defined* by his captivity and torture; and he opened a way in himself for new beginnings that might—but not necessarily—involve the possibility of reconciliation with those who tortured him.

. What Marty realized was that reconciliation was not necessary for him to be liberated. Which raises again the question: "What is forgiveness?" Marty understood that forgiveness was not something he did *for* any other person. Rather it was his heart's decision not to be bound up in revenge and hatred. If there was any action in the word, it was in releasing himself from what he called "eating the silage of bitterness and resentment." He describes how so many times during his captivity he was reminded of Dante's *Inferno* and its depiction of two political allies who once lived in thirteenth-century Pisa, Archbishop Ruggieri degli Ubaldini and Count Ugolino della Gherardesca. The archbishop betrayed the count and cruelly sealed him and his sons and grandsons in the tower, where they starved to death. During his pilgrimage through Hell, Dante finds the count and the archbishop frozen together in one hole, with the count gnawing upon the archbishop's skull in his eternal hunger for vengeance.

For too long we have been taught that we must forgive those who have harmed us—especially when they *ask* for forgiveness. It doesn't seem to matter whether they are sincere or what their motives are: whether they are asking for forgiveness to be relieved of their own guilt, or to avoid a longer prison sentence, or, in the case of Wiesenthal's dying soldier, to "avoid the fires of hell." In April 2004, at a ceremony in Kigali, Rwanda, marking the ten-year anniversary of the genocide, one speaker assured all those who had asked for forgiveness for their crimes in the genocide that they would be forgiven and would "sit at the right hand of God." Those who refused to forgive the *genocidaires* for killing their children in front of them, butchering their kin, for hunting them like animals, would find themselves "burning in Hell" for refusing to forgive—one more burden on those already overburdened with nightmares, sorrow, poverty, and a loss that cannot be compensated.

Answering Wiesenthal's question—"Was my silence at the bedside of the dying Nazi wrong?"—André Stein wrote:

Can we, indeed, advocate forgiveness toward those who have committed crimes against humanity? ... The consequences of participating in genocidal acts must include dying with a guilty conscience.

Such a warning could be meaningful to those teetering between good and evil and those who insinuate that survivors be nobler than they can afford to be. We must stop dictating moral postures for the survivors. The opposite of forgiving is neither cruelty nor wallowing. It is a way of healing and honoring our pain and grief.

Forgiveness is not something that can be demanded, and perhaps it should not be sought. Forgiveness *is* a gift, and that gift is to *oneself*.

I'm not so sure that the person who forgives can even will that forgiveness when it is demanded or requested. In these stories, it was not the talk of forgiveness that mattered as much as it was the idea of reaching out as "one caring." Marty reached out during his captivity to his captors with the compassion that was so much a part of who he was. His fear was that the torture would kill in him that that he held as his "caring self." Simon Wiesenthal brushed away the flies from the dying soldier's head, and when he met the soldier's mother, "I kept silent rather than shatter her illusions about her dead son's inherent goodness." While she was still grieving herself, Mathilde Rathenau reached out to the mother of her son's killer. Bernadette Kabango "untied the chains" that bound her.

In my June 2006 meeting with President Paul Kagame, he expressed his concern that those who were targeted would become "bullied bullies," people whose lives are consumed by the desire for revenge—"gnawing upon the archbishop's skull in his eternal hunger for vengeance." Nowhere in any other country have such large numbers of perpetrators and those they targeted been forced to coexist as neighbors, coworkers, and at times as members of the same family. What is important for those who are survivors of genocide is not that we ask them to forgive the *genocidaires* and reconcile with them, but that we help the survivors to hold onto their "caring selves." And if

we must use the word "forgiveness," we need to understand that the act of forgiveness is an act of "radical self-
interest." When people have been grievously harmed,
instead of asking them to forgive the one who harmed
them, perhaps it would be wiser and far more constructive
to ask them to be open to life again, to learn to trust again,
and to treat all whom they meet with integrity, civility, and
compassion. They do not have to like the person who has
harmed them; they don't have to be that person's friend.
We must say to survivors:

> I hear you. I am here for you. I believe you.
> You are not in this alone.
> You did nothing to cause this.
> There are things you can do.

These cannot be mere words or empty promises. The
reparation and the financial aid must be there, and so must
the support and care be more than just platitudes.

The people who have committed these crimes against
humanity and caused such grievous harm will need to
stand humbled (not humiliated); to be held accountable;
to take full responsibility for their actions (no excuses or
blame-shifting); and to participate in whatever way is
possible to help keep this crime against humanity from
happening again. For those who were planners, instigators,
and perpetrators of the first order, this plan for prevention
would most likely involve lifelong imprisonment. For
many others playing various roles on the Bully Circle,

their return to community life is inevitable. The focus then needs to be on restoration, coexistence, and healing, not the adversarial process and punishment. A successful return will require the humility, the accountability, and a plan to make some form of restitution. Chicago educator Frank Tobin summed up this difficult transition: "You've done something terrible, but you are also a human being with a mind and a heart and a soul, and you've got to find a way to live beyond the worst thing you have ever done."

Letting go of the need for revenge does not reduce the horror of the deed, does not excuse it, tolerate it, cover it, or smother it. Survivors have looked horror in the face, called it by name, let it choke and enrage them, but eventually the anger must be experienced and expressed without the hatred. Vengeance has been tried for too long and has produced only more violence and revenge, and heartaches that don't go away—ever. What is needed instead is a way to "let go of the poison."

> But the words of my Seneca mother to me when I was badly wronged and wanted revenge and retaliation stay with me: "Do not be so ignorant and stupid and inhuman as they are. Go to the elder and ask for the medicine that will turn your heart from bitterness to sweetness. You must learn the wisdom of how to let go of poison.
>
> —SISTER JOSÉ HOBDAY

NEVER AGAIN?

Tears without action are wasted sentiment.

—JODI WILLIAMS,
NOBEL LAUREATE FOR PEACE, 1997

Is genocide inevitable? The short answer would seem to be "yes." Despite the vow of *Never Again*, genocides continue to occur, unabated, while the world watches, defining them instead as "deeply entrenched inevitabilities of economic/tribal/cultural/religious differences," or as the "collateral damage of armed conflict." Genocide is a reality today for the people of the Sudan, and the risk of genocide remains frighteningly real for people in other hot spots in the world.

With globalization, greed and self-interest, the failure of justice, the complicity of leaders, both secular and religious, is it possible to stop a genocide before it happens, to intervene effectively before it is too late? If the only responsibility that nations recognize is to pursue their own national self-interest, without seeing our connectedness, each to one another, then the answer given by Primo Levi in 1986 rings true today: "It happened, therefore it can happen again."

Can we instead create new roles, change the plot, reset the stage, and scrap the tragic ending? The actors can't do it alone. We, as an international community, have to get out of our seats—we can't afford to be passive, inattentive, bored, alarmed, or merely deeply saddened. We can't walk out, close the show, and send it somewhere else. We can't merely banish the bullies and mourn those targeted for extermination. It's the roles that must be abandoned—and the international community (on a global and local scale) must become an active participant in a total rewrite. Those who can guide us are the ones who in the face of other genocides were witnesses, resisters, and defenders, those who jumped onto the stage as the scripts were being written and sounded the alarm we refused to hear; the ones who refused to abandon those who were targeted; those who defied the *genocidaires*; and those who survived genocide and denied the *genocidaires* their victory.

UBUNTU

The most acute need is not for policies but for political will. So here is a suggestion: Let's charter a few cargo planes to carry the corpses of hundreds of new victims from Darfur and Chad to the U.N. The butchered victims of Darfur could lie in state as a memorial to global indifference—and as a spur to become serious about the first genocide of the 21st century.

—NICHOLAS D. KRISTOF, "WHEN GENOCIDE WORSENS"

With silent indifference, and a few tears, much of the world community turned a blind eye to the genocide of the Armenians, Jews, Roma and Sinti, and Tutsis—and once again to the Fur in Darfur. To do and to justify the unthinkable, to rank some humans as more human than others, and to pretend to care and never really care is to deny our common humanity.

Explaining the African concept of *ubuntu*, Archbishop Desmond Tutu noted that it means "I am me only because you are you; my humanity is caught up in your humanity. If I dehumanize you, I am inexorably dehumanized.... [C]oncern for others is the best form of self-interest." Each one of us depends on the well-being of the whole; if the "We" is diminished, each one of us is less. Genocide rips apart the fabric of our humanity, and, as Nicolas D. Kristof said, "The only way to assert our own humanity is to stand up to it." When individuals, families, communities, and nations stand up to it, leaders will no longer find support for the complicity that enables it.

We must no longer view hatred as natural, normal, or necessary; disparity in wealth as inevitable; or injustice as simply regrettable.

By studying the words and actions of those who not only did not succumb to the intoxicating madness around them but railed against it, and by studying conditions under which ordinary people commit extraordinary evil and attempting to comprehend that evil, it is possible to create conditions in our communities and in the world that will strengthen inhibitions against such violence and nurture those bonds that connect us, one to another. There is no "I" without a "Thou," no "We" without community, and no way to survive without honoring both our unique individuality and common humanity. Finding this common ground of honoring our unique individuality and common humanity is critical to the early prevention of genocide.

When we respond with a generous spirit, discernment, and mercy, when we help alleviate the suffering of others and offer them our compassion and loving-kindness, we create caring communities.

It is these caring communities, one by one, with leadership that recognizes its power to shape attitudes and lead people to action in ways that honor our common bond, our individuality, and our commonality that can make real the promise: "Never Again."

I remember: it happened yesterday, or eternities ago.
A young Jewish boy discovered the Kingdom of
Night. I remember his bewilderment, I remember his
anguish. It all happened so fast. The ghetto. The
deportation. The sealed cattle car. The fiery altar
upon which the history of our people and the future
of mankind were meant to be sacrificed.

I remember he asked his father, "Can this be true?
This is the twentieth century, not the Middle Ages.
Who would allow such crimes to be committed?
How could the world remain silent?"

And now the boy is turning to me. "Tell me," he
asks, "what have you done with my future, what have

you done with your life?" And I tell him I have tried. That I have tried to keep memory alive, that I have tried to fight those who would forget. Because if we forget, we are guilty, we are accomplices.

—ELIE WIESEL, NOBEL PEACE PRIZE
ACCEPTANCE SPEECH, DECEMBER 10, 1986

Notes

Epigraphs

p. vii   *"I am a survivor of a concentration camp"*: Chaim Ginott, from *Teacher and Child* (New York: Macmillan, 1972).

p. viii   *"It is not the function of history to drum ethical lessons"*: Gerda Lerner, *The Creation of Patriarchy* (New York: Oxford University Press, 1986).

Introduction *A Wall in Kigali*

p. xi   *"Nothing rips more at the common fabric of humanity"*: Nicholas D. Kristof, "Disposable Cameras for Disposable People," *New York Times*, February 12, 2006.

p. xv   "God's protection [that] ended instead in the arms of Lucifer": Roméo Dallaire, *Shake Hands with the Devil: The Failure of Humanity in Rwanda* (Toronto: Random House, 2003).

p. xvi   "threw their children into the water to spare them": African Rights, *Rwanda: Death, Despair and Defiance*, revised edition (London: African Rights, 1995), pp. 798–99.

p. xvii   *"Real ideas must as a rule be simplified to the level of a child's understanding"*: Sebastian Haffner, *Defying Hitler: A Memoir* (New York: Farrar, Straus and Giroux, 2002), p. 16.

p. xviii   "the death of his family ... the death of his innocence": publisher's description of Elie Wiesel's *Night* (New York: Farrar, Straus and Giroux Publishers, 2006).

p. xviii   "doesn't remove it from the realm of human nature or human comprehension": In R. Rosenbaum, *Explaining Hitler: The Search for the Origins of His Evil* (New York: Random House, 1998), p. 281.

p. xxii   Contact the Tumurere Foundation at tumurere@
          inbox.rwanda.

p. xxiv   *"Genocides are deadly to the victims"*: Eric D. Weitz, *A
          Century of Genocide: Utopias of Race and Nation* (Princeton,
          NJ: Princeton University Press, 2003), p. 252.

Chapter 1   Genocide: A Definition

p. 1   *"Quite obviously, if humanity is to develop sound conventions"*:
          Samuel Totten, "Wrestling with the Definition of
          'Genocide'" in *Teaching About Genocide: Issues, Approaches,
          and Resources*, Samuel Totten, Ed. (Greenwich, CT:
          Information Age Publications, 2004), p. 64.

p. 1   "The whole of Europe has been wrecked and trampled
          down": Winston Churchill, BBC Radio broadcast,
          August 24, 1941.

p. 2   Lemkin launched a personal drive to declare it a crime to
          destroy, in whole or in part: United Nations Convention
          on the Prevention and Punishment of the Crime of
          Genocide, adopted by Resolution 260 (III) A of the U.N.
          General Assembly on 9 December 1948. Entered into
          force 12 January 1951.

p. 3   "Acts of Barbarity and Vandalism": Additional explica-
          tions to the Special Report presented to the 5th
          Conference for the Unification of Penal Law in Madrid
          (14–20 October 1933).

p. 3   "While society sought protection against individual
          crimes": Raphäel Lemkin, *Axis Rule in Occupied Europe: Laws
          of Occupation, Analysis of Government, Proposals for Redress*
          (Washington: Carnegie Endowment for International
          Peace, Division of International Law, 1944).

p. 4   "Adding shading to an already sinister picture": Frank
          Chalk and Kurt Jonassohn, *The History and Sociology of
          Genocide: Analyses and Case Studies* (New Haven: Yale
          University Press, 1990), p. 271.

pp. 4–5   "Genocide is a denial of the right of existence of entire
          human groups": United Nations General Assembly,
          Resolution, 1946.

p. 9   "The [United Nations] Secretariat's mentality, how it was organized to think": Michael Barnett, *Eyewitness to a Genocide: The United Nations and Rwanda* (Ithaca: Cornell University Press, 2002).

p. 10   *"The human desire to 'right wrongs' is as old as recorded history."*: from *My Neighbor, My Enemy: Justice and Community in the Aftermath of Mass Atrocity*, Eric Stover and Harvey M. Weinstein, Eds. (Cambridge: Cambridge University Press, 2004), p. 10.

p. 11   "I am accused of genocide, but what does that mean?": Associated Press, January 31, 1997.

p. 12   "to coordinate and oversee the brutal ethnic separation campaign": Marlise Simons, "Wartime Leader of Bosnian Serbs Receives 27-Year Sentence," *New York Times*, September 28, 2006, A8.

p. 13   *"The ethical dimension of the word is such"*: Josias Semujanga, *Origins of Rwandan Genocide* (Amherst, N.Y. : Humanity Books, 2003), p. 246.

p. 13   *"If there is one thing sure in this world, it is certainly this"*: Primo Levi, *Survival in Auschwitz: The Nazi Assault on Humanity* (Cambridge: ProQuest Information and Learning, 2002).

p. 14   *"It happened, therefore it can happen again."*: Primo Levi, *The Drowned and the Saved* (New York: Vintage, 1989), p. 19.

p. 14   "has been exposed as a slogan, not a promise": William Shawcross, foreword to Alan Destexhe, *Rwanda and Genocide in the Twentieth Century* (New York: New York University Press, 1995).

p. 14   "the human reality of mass killings and genocide": James Waller, *Becoming Evil: How Ordinary People Commit Genocide and Mass Killing* (Oxford: Oxford University Press, 2002).

pp. 14–15   "If you don't protect the people of Darfur today": Peter Beinart quoting Freddy Umutanguha in "How to Save Darfur," *Time* magazine, September 24, 2006.

p. 15   "Never shall I forget that night": Wiesel, *Night*.

p. 16 "we must eliminate from this earth the impunity with which the genocidaires were able to act": Dallaire, *Shake Hands with the Devil*.

pp. 16–17 "A consequence of this kind of reasoning": Alain Destexhe, *Rwanda and Genocide in the Twentieth Century* (New York: New York University Press, 1995).

p. 18 "[I]f not, the real meaning of genocide will continue to be trivialized": Destexhe, *Rwanda and Genocide in the Twentieth Century*, p. 15.

p. 19 "is easy—and this is a vast understatement": Samuel Totten, quoted in Gerald Caplan, "The Genocide Problem: 'Never Again' All Over Again, Part II," *The Walrus* magazine, October 2004.

p. 19 "undertake to prevent and to punish" genocide perpetrators: Convention on the Prevention and Punishment of the Crime of Genocide, Adopted by Resolution 260 (III) A of the U.N. General Assembly on 9 December 1948. Entered into force: 12 January 1951.

p. 20 *"At the end of the day, no Geneva Convention on genocide"*: Caplan, "The Genocide Problem."

Chapter 2 Anatomy of Extraordinary Evil

p. 21 "Who, after all, speaks today of the annihilation of the Armenians?": Adolf Hitler, in a speech to his Supreme Commanders and Commanding Generals, Obersalzberg, Germany, August 22, 1939, quoted in Samantha Power, *A Problem From Hell: America and the Age of Genocide* (New York: Basic Books, 2002).

p. 22 "In all, he submitted to Berlin fifteen reports on the deportations and mass killings": Robert Fisk, *The Great War for Civilisation: The Conquest of the Middle East* (New York: Alfred A. Knopf, 2005), pp. 329–30.

p. 24 "It's no use for you to argue. We have already disposed of three quarters of the Armenians": Mehmed Talaat, quoted in Richard Hovannisian, *Armenia on the Road to Independence 1918* (Berkeley: University of California Press, 1967), p. 52.

p. 24   *"Each bloodletting hastens the next"*: President Bill Clinton, Rwanda, March 25, 1998, see http://www.clinton foundation.org/legacy/032598-speech-by-president-to-survivors-rwanda.htm.

p. 25   *"All rights of the Armenians such as to live and work on Turkish soil"*: Talaat Bey, Turkish minister of Internal Affairs, in confidential correspondence dated September 9, 1915, addressed to the governor general of Aleppo, quoted in Naim Bey, *The Memoirs of Naim Bey: Turkish Official Documents Relating to the Deportations and Massacres of Armenians* (Newton Square, PA: Armenian Historical Research Association, 1964).

p. 26   "note of macabre effrontery": Abram L. Sachar, in his foreword to Richard G. Hovannesian, *The Armenian Holocaust* (Cambridge: Armenian Heritage Press, 1978), p.xi.

p. 26   Talaat asked American Ambassador, Henry Morgenthau for "a list of Armenians who had been insured by American firms": Henry Morgenthau, *Ambassador Morgenthau's Story* (Detroit: Wayne State University Press, 2003) p. 233.

p. 27   *"No assessment of modern culture"*: Irving Greenberg in Frank Chalk and Kurt Jonassohn, *The History and Sociology of Genocide: Analyses and Case Studies* (New Haven, CT: Yale University Press, 1990).

p. 28   *"We ... say to the* Inyenzi *[cockroaches]"*: Hassan Ngeze, *Kangura* magazine, January 1994.

p. 29   *"Armenians cannot easily forget those earlier horrors"*: V. L. Parsegian, *Human Rights and Genocide, 1975: The Hope, the Reality, and Still the Hope* (New York: Diocese of the Armenian Church of America, 1975).

p. 30   *"It must be discomforting to come to grips"*: Daniel N. Paul, *First Nations History: We Were Not The Savages—Collision Between European and Native American Civilizations* (Black Point, NS: Fernwood Books, 2006).

p. 31   "must by reconciled and viewed together": Taner Akçam, *A Shameful Act: The Armenian Genocide and the Question of Turkish Responsibility* (New York: Metropolitan Books, 2006), p. 13.

p. 31   "two legitimate sides": Peter Balakian, *The Burning Tigris: The Armenian Genocide and America's Response* (New York: HarperCollins, 2003).

pp. 32–33   Richard G. Hovannisian lists the similarities between the genocide of the Armenians and the genocide of the Jews: Richard G. Hovannisian, *The Armenian Holocaust: A Bibliography Relating to the Deportations, Massacres, and Dispersion of the Armenian People, 1915–1923* (Cambridge, MA: Armenian Heritage Press, 1978), p. xv.

p. 34   *"[T]he Armenian massacre was the greatest crime of the war"*: President Theodore Roosevelt in a, letter to Cleveland H. Dodge, May 11, 1918.

pp. 34–35   *"As Lemkin noted, war and genocide are almost always connected"*: Power, *A Problem From Hell*, pp. 90–91.

p. 35   a 1999 research project done by Simon and Chabris: Daniel J. Simons and Christopher F. Chabris, *Gorillas in Our Midst: Sustained Inattentional Blindness for Dynamic Events. Perception* 1999, vol. 28, 1059–74.

p. 36   "Any abuses were fairly typical if 'regrettable' features of war": Talaat Pasha, *Memoirs*, published 1921.

p. 37   "The Sublime Porte intends to make use of the world war": Talaat Pasha, *Memoirs*, published 1921.

p. 37   "I was told that, in various quarters of Aleppo": Dr. Martin Niepage, *The Armenian Genocide: Dr. Martin Piege's Report* (Plandome NY: New Age Publishers, 1975), p. 1.

p. 37   "The aim of war is not to reach definite lines": Adolf Hitler, quoted in Power, *A Problem From Hell*.

p. 38   "A punishment is being meted out": Joseph Goebbels, *"Der Jude," Der Angriff* (January 21, 1928), pp. 323–24.

p. 39   "Personally, I don't believe in the genocide": Stanislas Mbonampeka, quoted in Philip Gourevitch, *We Wish To Inform You That Tomorrow We Will Be Killed with Our Families* (New York: Farrar, Straus and Giroux, 1998).

p. 40   "If you have major problems with the guidance provided above": in Dallaire, *Shake Hands with the Devil*.

p. 41   "There was the plain fact that the RPF and the government had resumed war": Barnett, *Eyewitness to a Genocide*, pp. 103, 120.

p. 43   "its troops began to discover massacre sites": Colin M. Waugh, *Paul Kagame and Rwanda: Power, Genocide and the Rwandan Patriotic Front* (Jefferson, NC: McFarland and Co., 2004), p. 68.

p. 43   Oxfam was the first organization to call it what it was: Dallaire, *Shake Hands with the Devil.*

p. 44   "warring parties do not reach an agreement on a cease-fire": "UN Troops Pray as They Scramble out of Rwanda," *The Toronto Star,* April 21, 1994, A5.

p. 44   the United States issued a presidential directive: *The Clinton Administration's Policy on Reforming Multilateral Peace Operations,* see http://www.gwu.edu/~nsarchiv/NSAEBB/NSAEBB53/rw050094.pdf.

p. 45   In a press conference on June 10, 1994: U.S. Department of State, Daily Press Briefing, June 10, 1994.

p. 46   "As a responsible government, you don't just go round hollering 'genocide'": Douglas Jehl, "Official Told to Avoid Calling Rwanda Killings 'Genocide,'" *New York Times,* June 10, 1994, A8.

p. 47   "They trust in goodfaith negotiations and traditional diplomacy": Power, *A Problem from Hell.*

p. 47   "There were two things the UN could have done": Destexhe, *Rwanda and Genocide in the Twentieth Century,* p. 51.

p. 48   "The strictly humanitarian character of this operation ... shall be conducted": United Nations Security Council Resolution 929, 22 June 1994.

p. 50   *"The [UN Security] council saw the situation in Rwanda":* Barnett, *Eyewitness to a Genocide,* p. 103.

Chapter 3   *Genocide: Bullying to the Extreme*

p. 51   *"Hate has a nearly limitless ability to dehumanize its victims":* Rush W. Dozier, Jr., *Why We Hate: Understanding, Curbing, and Eliminating Hate in Ourselves and Our World* (Chicago : Contemporary Books, 2002).

p. 53   *"Mass killing or genocide is usually the outcome":* Ervin Staub, "The Psychology of Bystanders, Perpetrators, and Heroic

Helpers," *International Journal of Intercultural Relations*, 17, no. 3 (Summer 1993), 315–41.

p. 53   "atrocity producing situations": Robert Jay Lifton, "Conditions of Atrocity,"in *The Nation*, May 31, 2004.

p. 54   "the discursive inferno of civil war": Barnett, *Eyewitness to a Genocide*, p. 50.

p. 58   "If three Jews robbed a bank": Fritz Stern, *Five Germanys I Have Known* (New York: Farrar, Straus and Giroux, 2006).

p. 59   "The Armenian vermin gathered tonight": Archive of the Armenian Patriarchate of Jerusalem, box 21, dossier M, document no. 511.

p. 61   "arrogance that has been mortally wounded": Lawrence Terzian, *Perseverence: Ara Baliozian and the Armenian Cause* (Kitchener: Impressions, 1990), p. 73.

p. 61   "international Jewry froths at the mouth": Joseph Goebbels, April 19, 1945, diary entry.

p. 62–63   "Having planted their swords in the ground, blade up": Aurora Mardiganian, *Ravished in Armenia*, quoted in Peter Balakian, *The Burning Tigris: The Armenian Genocide and America's Response* (New York: HarperCollins, 2003), p. 262.

p. 63   "Evil that arises out of ordinary thinking": Ervin Staub, *The Roots of Evil* (Cambridge: Cambridge University Press, 1989), p. 126.

p. 66   "out of circulation" was not terror but "social hygiene": Joseph Goebbels *"Der Jude,"* pp. 323–24.

p. 66   "We the people are obliged to take responsibility ourselves to wipe out this scum": Gourevitch, *We Wish to Inform You*, pp. 96–97.

p. 66   an advisor to the President of the Democratic Republic of the Congo called for the Tutsi "vermin to be eradicated": Already, on August 4, 1998, according to testimony quoted in the International Arrest warrant, Mr. Yerodia Ndombasi had spoken on RTNC radio about *"de vermine qu'il fallait éradiquer avec méthode."*

p. 67   *"The contempt for my people—every assumption, insult, and slur"*: Carl Upchurch, *Convicted in the Womb: One Man's*

Journey from Prison to Peacemaker (New York: Bantam Books, 1996).

pp. 68–69   "*[Armenian women] were holding hands and walking in a circle*": Peter Balakian, *Black Dog of Fate: An American Son Uncovers His Armenian Past* (New York: Basic Books, 1997).

p. 72   "destroys the fundamental fabric and interpersonal relations": African Rights, *Rwanda*, p. 749.

p. 72   "[T]he Turks have been taking their choice of these children": Leslie A. Davis to Ambassador Henry Morgenthau, in Donald E. Miller and Lorna Touryan Miller, *Survivors: An Oral History of the Armenian Genocide* (Berkeley: University of California Press, 1993), pp. 20–24.

p. 72   "The guards ... were the worst abusers": Reverend F. H. Leslie, in Miller and Miller, *Survivors*, pp. 20-24.

p. 73   "*Since antiquity there was a twisted code of conduct*": R. G. Hovannisian, "The Armenian Genocide," in Samuel Totten, Ed., *Teaching About Genocide: Issues, Approaches, and Resources* (Greenwich, CT: Information Age Publications, 2004) , p. 105.

p. 73   "*Cruelty is social in its origin*": Zygmunt Bauman, *Modernity and the Holocaust* (Ithaca, NY: Cornell University Press, 1989), p. 166.

p. 74   "a six-foot Turk, with a two-foot knife in his hand": Kerop Bedoukian, *Some of Us Survived: The Story of an Armenian Boy* (New York: Farrar, Straus, and Giroux, 1979).

pp. 74–75   "Cruelties had already been committed, but so far not too publicly": Alma Johannsen, quoted in Miller and Miller, *Survivors*, pp. 20–24.

pp. 75–76   "That was apparently left to the intiative of the company captains": Christopher Browning, *Ordinary Men, Reserve Police Battalion 101 and The Final Solution in Poland* (New York: HarperCollins, 1992).

p. 77   "Methodically and with much bravado and laughter": Dallaire, *Shake Hands with the Devil*, p. 280.

p. 78   "the spontaneous outburst of an enraged nation": Martin Gilbert, *Kristallnacht: A Prelude to Destruction* (New York: HarperCollins, 2006).

p. 78   "The Nazis burned all the books in the streets, and also
         the Torah": Miriam Walk, in Gilbert, *Kristallnacht*.

p. 79   "were not different in their moral makeup": Raul Hilberg,
         The Destruction of the European Jews (Chicago: Quadrangle
         Books, 1961).

pp. 79–80 "[A] psychiatrist examined him and pronounced him
           perfectly sane": Thomas Merton, *Raids on the Unspeakable*
           (New York: New Directions, 1966).

p. 80   "It came as no surprise to me": Caplan, "The Genocide
         Problem."

p. 80   *"It is not the murderer in Stangle that terrifies us"*: Elie
         Wiesel, back jacket copy to Gitta Sereny, *Into That
         Darkness* (New York: Random House, 1983).

p. 80   "banality of evil": Hannah Arendt, *Eichmann in Jerusalem:
         A Report on the Banality of Evil* (New York: Viking, 1963).

Chapter 4   *Three Characters and a Tragedy*

p. 81   *"We used to think that if we knew one"*: Arthur Eddington, in
         N. Rose, *Mathematical Maxims and Minims* (Raleigh, NC:
         Rome Press Inc., 1988).

p. 82   An illustrated adaptation of the Bullying Circle developed
         by Dan Olweus, Ph.D., of the University of Bergen,
         Norway, one of the world's leading researchers on bullying
         and peer harassment. He has developed a highly successful
         intervention program in Bergen that has proven to signifi-
         cantly reduce bullying in schools throughout the world
         that have adopted it. Information on Olweus's Core
         Program Against Bullying and Antisocial Behavior can be
         obtained from olweus@online.no or Dan Olweus, Ph.D.,
         Research Center for Health Promotion, Christiesgate 13,
         N-5015 Bergen, Norway (phone: 011-47-55-58-23-27).

p. 85   "It is even worse that comradeship relieves men of respon-
         sibility": Haffner, *Defying Hitler*, pp. 285–86.

pp. 86–87 "There's no inherent human nature that requires us to kill
           or maim": Interview with Dr. Robert Jay Lifton, found at
           http://www.democracynow.org/article.pl?sid=06/06/12/13
           20246&mode=thread&tid=25.

p. 87   *"It is immensely moving when a mature man"*: Max Weber, "Politics as a Vocation," in Max Weber, H. H. Gerth, and C. Wright Mills, *From Max Weber: Essays in Sociology* (New York: Oxford University Press, 1958).

p. 87   *"If only there were evil people somewhere"*: Alexander Solzhenitsyn, *The Gulag Archipelago* (New York: Harper and Roe, 1974).

p. 90   In one of his most infamous speeches he exhorted his audience to "rise up": "Propaganda and Practice," Human Rights Watch: http://www.hrw.org/reports/1999/rwanda/Geno1-3-10.htm.

p. 91   *"The road to Auschwitz was built by hatred"*: Ian Kershaw, "The Persecution of the Jews and German Public Opinion in the Third Reich," *Leo Baeck Institute Yearbook 26* (1981), p. 288.

p. 91   *"It is true that we Armenians have lost much"*: An Armenian ecclesiastic at a "reconciliation banquet" held after the 1909 massacre of Armenians.

p. 92   The "gray zone of *protekcya* [corruption] and collaboration": Primo Levi, "The Gray Zone" in *The Drowned and the Saved* (New York: Summit Books, 1988).

p. 92   "It is naïve and absurd to believe": Levi, *The Drowned and the Saved.*

pp. 93–95   "After about fifteen minutes of bitter sobbing": M. Birnbaum, Y. Rosenblum, *Lieutenant Birnbaum: A Soldier's Story* (Brooklyn, NY: Mesorah Publications, 1993), pp. x–xi.

p. 95   "Provocateurs, oppressors, all those who in some way injure others, are guilty": Levi, "The Gray Zone."

p. 96   "I would lightheartedly absolve all those whose concurrence in guilt was minimal and for whom coercion was of the highest degree": Levi, "The Gray Zone."

p. 96   *"The person who is induced into participation"*: J. M. Darley, "Social Organization for the Production of Evil," *Psychological Inquiry* 1992, 3, 209.

p. 98   "Such neutrality is derisory for it works against the weaker party": François-René de Chateaubriand.

p. 100   "Indifference finally grows lethal": Cynthia Ozick, Prologue to Gay Block and Malka Drucker, *Rescuers: Portraits of Moral Courage in the Holocaust* (New York: Holmes and Meier, 1992).

p. 102   *"Evil is not simply the result of a decision":* Stephen L. Carter, *Integrity* (New York: Basic Books, 1996).

p. 103   "It was constantly impressed upon me in forceful terms": Rudolph Höss and Steven Paskully, Ed., *Death Dealer: The Memoirs of the SS Kommandant at Auschwitz* (Buffalo: Promethus Books, 1992).

p. 103   *"Far more , and far more hideous, crimes have been committed":* C. P. Snow, quoted in Stanley Milgram, *Obedience to Authority: An Experimental View* (New York: Harper and Row, 1974).

p. 103   "We can learn more by looking": Herbert Kellman, "Violence without Moral Restraint: Reflections on the Dehumanization of Victims and Victimizers, *Journal of Social Issues* 1989, 29, 4.

p. 104   "Unquestioning obedience to authority that relieved the killers of personal responsibility": Kellman, "Violence without Moral Restraint."

p. 104   "when acts of violence are explicitly ordered": Kellman, "Violence without Moral Restraint."

p. 105   "I am a soldier, [the nation] is my commander": Ziya Gökalp in Uriel Heyd, *Foundations of Turkish Nationalism: The Life and Teachings of Ziya Gökalp* (London: Luzac, 1950), p. 29.

pp. 105–6   "The Commandments of the National Socialists": from *Handbook for Hitler Youth*, translated by Rudi Florian.

p. 106   "have blind faith in victory!": Joseph Goebbels, "Nr. 26, 4.6.44—Nürnberg, Adolf-Hitler-Platz (Hauptmarkt)"—in 1939–45, vol. 2 of Helmut Heiber, ed., *Goebbels-Reden* (Dusseldorf: Droste Verlag, 1972) pp. 340–41.

p. 107   "You take a poor, ignorant population": Francois Xavier Nkurunziza, speaking to Gourevitch, *We Wish to Inform You That Tomorrow*, p. 23.

p. 110   "Brutally dragged out of their native land ": see correspondence of September 10, 1916, at http://www.gomidas.org/gida/index_and_%20documents/867.4016_index_and_documents/docs/4016.302.pdf.

p. 111   "The SS made us increase our pace": Elie Wiesel, *Night*, p. 85.

p. 111   "are not like you and me": Rudolph Höss and Steven Paskully, ed., *Death Dealer: The Memoirs of the SS Kommandant at Auschwitz* (Buffalo: Promethus Books, 1992).

pp. 113–14   "The Ten Commandments of the Comittee of Union and Progress": Vahakn N. Dadrian analyzed the following document in his treatise "The Secret Young Turk Ittihadist Conference and the Decision for the World War I Genocide of the Armenians," in *Holocaust and Genocide Studies* 7, no. 2 (Fall 1993), 173–74. The original document was issued at a conference presided over by Talaat Pasha, and Drs. Nazim and Behaeddin Shakir.

pp. 114–15   "I have often in my lifetime been a prophet": Max Domarus, ed., *Hitler: Reden und Proklamationen*, vol. 2, *Untergang, 1939–1945* (Neustadt: Schmidt, 1962), pp. 1055–66; quotations on p. 1055. Hitler used the term *Vernichtung*, or "annihilation," of the Jewish race in Europe.

p. 117   "Here the Jews crouch among one another": Joseph Goebbels, quoted in James M. Glass, *Life Unworthy of Life: Racial Phobia and Mass Murder in Hitler's Germany* (New York: Basic Books, 1997).

pp. 118–20   "The Hutu Ten Commandments": published in *Kangura*, 10 December 1990.

p. 120   "because they share the cultural and institutional values on which they believe the state to be founded." Herbert C. Kelman and V. Lee Hamilton, *Crimes of Obedience* (New Haven: Yale University Press, 1989).

pp. 121–22   "doing the decent thing": in Hudson Talbott, *Forging Freedom: A True Story of Heroism During the Holocaust* (New York: G. P. Putnam's Sons, 2000).

pp. 122–23   *"Those who refused to obey the orders of the authorities"*: F. Rochat and A. Modigliani, "The Ordinary Quality of

Resistance: From Milgram's laboratory to the village of Le Chambon," *Journal of Social Issues*, 51, 195–210.

p. 125 "saved several thousand Jews": Ervin Staub, *The Roots of Evil: The Origins of Genocide and Other Group Violence* (New York: Cambridge University Press, 1989).

p. 126 "You can't let people in need down": Preben Munch-Nielson, posted at the Holocaust Museum in Washington, D.C.

pp. 127–28 *"To smuggle a loaf of bread was to resist":* Posted at the Ghetto Fighters' House, Israel.

p. 128 "We who lived in concentration camps can remember": Viktor Frankl, *Man's Search for Meaning: An Introduction to Logotherapy* (New York: Simon and Schuster, 1984).

p. 129 "the resolute intervention by Turkish officials": Pierre Vidal-Naquet, Preface to People's Permanent Tribunal, *A Crime of Silence: The Armenian Genocide* (London: Zed Books, Ltd, 1985).

p. 129 "In the Jebel Musa, or Musa Dadh, the Armenians refused to submit": Yves Ternon, quoted in Peter Sourian's Introduction to Franz Werfel, *The Forty Days of Musa Dagh* (New York: Viking, 1967).

pp. 130–31 "By late June, only about 2000 emaciated people were still alive": African Rights, *Resisting Genocide, Bisesero, April–June 1994* (London: African Rights, 1998), p. 2.

p. 131 "It was pointed out to me that there was value in our continued presence": Dr. Martin Niepiege, *The Horrors of Aleppo Seen by a German Eyewitness*, (London: T. F. Unwin, 1917), p. 3.

p. 133 "Accounts from different sources agree": Viscount James Bryce, "Bryce Asks U.S. to Aid Armenia," *New York Times*, September 21, 1915.

p. 134 "Deportation of and excesses against peaceful Armenians": Morgenthau, *Ambassador Morgenthau's Story.*

pp. 134–135 "by passive observation of this murder of defenseless millions": see David S. Wyman, *The Abandonment of the Jews: America and the Holocaust, 1941–1945* (New York: Pantheon, 1984).

pp. 135–36   "In 1944 at the age of ten": Rudi Florian, New Mexico Holocaust and Intolerance Museum pamphlet, 2006.

p. 137   *"Life and study have persuaded me of the openness of history"*: Stern, *The Five Germanys I Have Known*, p. 10.

Chapter 5   The Bully Circle

p. 138   *"The historical evidence on the spontaneity, inventiveness, and enthusiasm"*: Leonard S. Newman, Ralph Erber, eds., *Understanding Genocide* (New York: Oxford University Press, 2002), p. 100.

pp. 142   "The extremists' propaganda presented an alternative morality": African Rights, *Rwanda*.

p. 142   "I brought up the subject with my Mother": Hasmig Kurdian, from personal correspondence with the author.

p. 143   *"Though we want to believe that violence"*: Gavin de Becker, *The Gift of Fear: Survival Signals That Protect Us from Violence* (Boston: Little, Brown, 1997).

p. 143   *"Injustice anywhere is a threat to justice everywhere"*: Martin Luther King, Jr., *Letter from Birmingham Jail*, see http://www.almaz.com/nobel/peace/MLK-jail.html.

pp. 144–45   "It is true the ultimate responsibility for the plan": Kersam Aharonian, *A Historical Survey of the Armenian Case* (Watertown, Mass: Baikar Publications, 1989), pp. 61–62.

pp. 145–46   "I was twelve years old in 1915": Zakar Berberian, as told to Robert Fisk, *The Great War for Civilization: The Conquest of the Middle East* (New York: Alfred A. Knopf, 2005), p. 319.

pp. 147–51   "Before the war broke out, 1,600 Jews": Witness Szmul Wasersztajn, Jewish Historical Institute in Warsaw, collection no. 301, document no. 152 (301/152).

pp. 152–54   "My Father, who was born in 1907, must have been 7 or around 8": Hasmig Kurdian, from personal correspondence with the author.

pp. 154–62   "Life Was Useless for Tutsis in Rwanda During the Genocide": Isaie Munyaneza, from personal correspondence with the author.

pp. 162–68   "The attitude of the peasants toward the Jews was very bad": Menachem Finkelsztajn, Voivodeship Jewish Historical Commision, ZIH, 301/974.

p. 168   *"The voice of conscience and humanity will never be silenced in me":* Armin T. Wegner, in an open letter to President Wilson, Berlin, January 1919.

p. 168   *"Germany is nothing. Each individual German is everything":* Goethe, 1808.

p. 169   *"The power of choosing between good and evil is within the reach of all."* Origen (c. 185–254)

p. 170   "The city authority's doctor, Dr. Chboukdjyan from Constantinople": Samuel H. Zorian, *This Man and the Others: The Personal Memoirs of Samuel H. Zorian,* (London: Mihran & Azniv Essefian Charitable Trust, 1996), p. 13.

p. 172   "Jewish doctors were put on the backs of open trucks": John Cornwell, *Hitler's Scientists: Science, War, and the Devil's Pact* (New York: Viking, 2003), pp. 155–57.

p. 173   *"There must have been a moment at the beginning, where we all could have said no.":* Tom Stoppard, from *Rosencrantz and Guildenstern Are Dead, Jumpers, Travesties, Arcadia* (London: Faber and Faber, 2000).

p. 174   *"We stand with you ... in your proclamation of 'Never Again'":* Rwanda's President Paul Kagame, speaking at the official launch of the Interfaith Action for Peace in Africa (IFAPA). Monday June 19, 2006 , see http://www.gov.rw/government/president/speeches/2006/19_06_06_faith.html.

p. 174   "that Christian values of solidarity": African Rights, *Rwanda,* p. 923.

p. 175   "in-group morality" and "out-group hostility": John Hartung, "Love Thy Neighbor: The Evolution of In-Group Morality," *Skeptic,* 3, no. 4, 1995.

p. 176   "The first thing to do is rescue [Germany] from the Jew who is ruining our country": Adolf Hitler, quoted in Alan Bullock, *Hitler, a Study in Tyranny* (New York: Harper & Row, 1962).

p. 177   "There are some things that can be done so long as they are not discussed": Raul Helberg, *The Destruction of the*

European Jews (revised and definitive edition) (New York: Holmes and Meier, 1985).

pp. 177–78   "Adolf Hitler! We are united with you alone!": see Dr. Thomas Schirrmacher "National Socialism as Religion" at http://www.contra-mundum.org/schirrmacher/NS_Religion.pdf.

p. 180   *"If people are good only because they fear punishment":* Albert Einstein, "Einstein Revealed," *Nova* (DVD), 1996.

Chapter 6   Scenes from a Tragedy

p. 181   *"We worry that explaining Evil condones it":* Dan Wegner, quoted in "Yet Another Worry for Those Who Believe the Glass is Half-Empty," *New York Times*, Tuesday, January 9, 2007; see http://skeptacles.blogspot.com/2007/01/nyt-yet-another-worry-for-those-who.html.

p. 187   *"The massive trauma inflicted on the collective consciousness of the Armenian people":* Donald Bloxham, *The Great Game of Genocide* (Oxford: Oxford University Press, 2005).

pp. 187–88   "[Denial] is among the surest indicators of further genocidal massacres": Gregory H. Stanton "Eight Stages of Genocide" (originally written in 1996 at the Department of State; presented at the Yale University Center for International and Area Studies in 1998), see http://www.genocidewatch.org/8stages.htm.

p. 188   "a struggle between two nations for the possession of a single homeland": Bernard Lewis, *The Emergence of Modern Turkey* (New York: Oxford University Press, 2002).

p. 188   "The majority of those who were deported survived": Justin McCarthy, "The Other Side of the Falsified Genocide," see http://www.tallarmeniantale.com/mccarthy-historian-decide.htm.

p. 188   "You cannot use that word genocide": Francois Karera, quoted in Jane Perlez "Under the Bougainvillea, A Litany of Past Wrongs," *The New York Times* on the Web, August 15, 1994, see http://partners.nytimes.com/library/world/africa/081594rwanda-genocide.html.

p. 188   "If we are able to demonstrate effectively that six million Jews were not 'gassed'": Lewis Brandon, in *The Journal of Historical Review* (Summer 1980).

p. 189   "It was not war. It was most certainly massacre and genocide": Israeli Foreign Minister Yossi Bielin, in the Knesset, April 27, 1994. Quoted in *Carina Karakashian* "87th Anniversary of Armenian Genocide Commemorated on Campus" at http://armenianstudies.csufresno.edu/hye_sharzhoom/vol23/may2002/genocide.htm.

p. 189   "National Day of Remembrance of Man's Inhumanity to Man": U.S. House of Representatives Joint Resolution 148, April 9, 1975.

p. 189   "the ambiguous facts of the massacres": Andrew Corsun, "Armenian Terrorism: A Profile," *Department of State Bulletin* (August 1982), pp. 31–35.

p. 189   "The only question for the U.S. is what's our national interest": Ambassador John Bolton, speech before the Global Structures Convocation in New York, February 3, 1994.

pp. 190–91   "There are always deniers": Gerry Caplan, "The Rwandan Genocide 12 Years Later—No Lessons Learned," *The Globe and Mail*, April 10, 2006.

p. 191   "vitriolic actions of those who are bad": Martin Luther King, Jr., *The Autobiography of Martin Luther King, Jr.* (New York: Intellectual Properties Management in association with Warner Books, 1998).

p. 192   "This is a popular saying": Deran Rushton-Zorian, translating his father's story, *This Man and the Others: The Personal Memoirs of Samuel H. Zorian*, (London: Mihran and Azniv Essefian Charitable Trust, 1996) p. 72.

p. 193   "When people proclaim that the past is not worth remembering": Arnold J. Toynbee, in *Toynbee on Toynbee: A Conversation Between Arnold J. Toynbee and G.R. Urban* (New York: Oxford University Press, 1974), pp. 48, 50, 68.

Chapter 7   *Restoring Community*

p. 194   *"Criminal prosecution after the fact doesn't effectively prevent atrocity":* Mark Drumbl, National Public Radio, September 28, 2006.

p. 196   "In one way or another, as a supporter, as a perpetrator, as a victim": Archbishop Demond Tutu, *No Future without Forgiveness* (New York: Doubleday, 1999).

p. 197   "The survivor cannot stop himself from permanently going back to the genocide": Jean-Baptiste Munyankore, in an interview with Jean Hatzfeld, *Into the Quick of Life: The Survivors Speak: A Report* (London: Serpent's Tail, 2005), p. 43.

pp. 197–98   "In grief unspeakable, I give you my hand—you of all women the most pitiable": first published in *Harper's*, April 1943; reprinted in Rabbi Joseph Telushkin, *Jewish Wisdom: Ethical, Spiritual, and Historical Lessons from the Great Works and Thinkers* (New York: W. Morrow, 1994).

p. 198   "There is now a crack in my life": Jean Hatzfeld, *Machete Season: The Killers in Rwanda Speak* (New York: Farrar, Straus, and Giroux, 2005) pp. 192–93.

pp. 199–201   "The Killers": Bernadette Kabango—given to author by poet, December 2006.

p. 201   "We who suffered in those dreadful days": Simon Wiesenthal, *The Sunflower, On the Possibilities and Limits of Forgiveness* (New York: Schocken Books, 1976).

pp. 202–3   "Was my silence at the bedside of the dying Nazi wrong?": Wiesenthal, *The Sunflower* (1998 edition).

p. 203   "just as much as it once challenged my heart and my mind": Wiesenthal, *The Sunflower*.

p. 204   "*I forgive, but I remember*": Father Martin Lawrence Jenco, *Bound to Forgive: The Pilgrimage to Reconciliation of a Beirut Hostage* (Notre Dame, IN: Ave Maria Press, 1995).

p. 204   "I am liberated. I need no longer be determined by the past": Jenco, *Bound to Forgive*.

pp. 206–7   "Can we, indeed, advocate forgiveness toward those who have committed crimes": André Stein in Wiesenthal, *The Sunflower*, p. 253.

pp. 209   "*But the words of my Seneca mother to me when I was badly wronged*": Sister José Hobday in Wiesenthal, *The Sunflower* (1998 edition), p. 174–75.

p. 210 "It happened, therefore it can happen again": Levi, *The Drowned and the Saved.*

p. 211 *"The most acute need is not for policies but for political will":* Nicholas D. Kristof, "When Genocide Worsens," *New York Times,* July 9, 2006, op ed., p. 12.

p. 212 "I am me only because you are you": Desmond Mpilo Tutu, *No Future without Forgiveness* (New York: Image Doubleday, 1999).

p. 212 "the only way to assert our own humanity is to stand up to it": Kristof, "Disposable Cameras for Disposable People."

pp. 213–14 *"I remember: it happened yesterday, or eternities ago":* Elie Wiesel, the Nobel Peace Prize acceptance speech delivered in Oslo, December 10, 1986.

Acknowledgments

My heartfelt thanks to the following:

David Davidar, publisher of Penguin Group (Canada), for coming up with the concept for this book and asking me to write it. You helped me to put to paper thirty years of observation, investigation, and reflection.

Stephen Lewis, the United Nations' special envoy for HIV/AIDS in Africa, for reintroducing me to Africa in general and Rwanda in particular, and for giving me the opportunity to meet General Roméo Dallaire and Gerry Caplan—two men whose work has greatly influenced mine. I cherish our friendship and am inspired by your passion and compassion.

Gerry Caplan, for sharing your time, your thoughts, and your writing with me. Your probing questions have pushed me to question more deeply the roles individuals, organizations, and countries play in genocide. Your writing gives voice to those who were silenced.

Shyrna Gilbert, who founded Hope for Rwanda, for introducing me to the dedicated people of the Tumerere Foundation and the young people who were orphaned in the genocide of 1994. Your commitment to educating young people in Canada and Rwanda is an inspiration to me.

Salpi Ger Ghazarian, executive director of AGBU in Toronto, for sharing your family's story and for introducing me to Hasmig Kurdian.

Hasmig Kurdian, for sharing your family's story, for keeping me up to date on the political struggle for recognition of the genocide of the Armenians, for introducing me to great historians whose writing has influenced this book, and for introducing me to Hovsep Torossian, who in turn introduced me to the enduring history of the Armenians.

Judith Cohen, a survivor of a death camp during the genocide of the Jews during World War II, who is today passionately pushing for action to stop the genocide in Darfur. You are truly a resister, a defender, and a witness. I thank you for your inspiration.

Rudi Florian, for translating the excerpt from the handbook for Hitler Youth and for sharing your story of escaping the tentacles of the movement and your subsequent commitment to human rights work.

Paul Kagame, president of Rwanda, for reading my book on bullying and taking the time to talk with me about its relevance to the genocide in Rwanda. You saw the "gorilla in our midst" and responded to it swiftly with courage and deep conviction.

Agnes Binagwaho, physician and head of the National AIDS Council of Rwanda, for introducing me to PACFA (Protection and Care for Families against HIV/AIDS) and giving me another way to make a small difference in the lives of the families in Rwanda.

Odette Nyiramilimo, senator and physician, for sharing a piece of your family's story and helping me to see the enormousness and complexity of the task of rebuilding a country in the aftermath of genocide.

Janvier Ntalinda, the man who speaks five languages and seems to know almost everyone in Rwanda, for making it so easy to quickly get involved in the world of children and youth impacted by the genocide. Your energy and enthusiasm is contagious. If only all of your knowledge was.

Michael Kalisa, legal assistant for the genocide trials in Arusha, for introducing me to and walking me through the Rwandan legal system and Gacaca.

Bernadette Kabango, for sharing your poem "The Killers," which graphically recreates the horrors inflicted on entire families by the *genocidaires*.

Isaie Munyaneza, for sharing your story of the genocide of the Tutsi and for denying the *genocidaires* a victory by not only surviving, but by thriving and reaching out to others with deep caring. You, Clarissa, and David are a gift to our family.

Barbara Berson, senior editor at Penguin Group (Canada), for your personal commitment to this book, your keen eye, and probing questions, and most of all for your persistence when I was ready to abandon the writing project. I am grateful for your support and friendship through the writing of five of my books.

Catherine Marjoribanks, once again for your attention to detail, consistency, and structure—and your humorous e-mails that helped lift my spirit when I was discouraged.

Patrick Crean, my literary agent, for your insights, knowledge of history and literature, and suggested readings, and most of all for your encouragement every step of the way.

Sandra Tooze, for again orchestrating the production of the book and bringing together such talented people as proofreader Karen Alliston, formatter Christine Gambin, fact checker Jennifer Howse, and cold reader Dawn Hunter.

Satomi Morii, for introducing me to a Japanese perspective of the bombing of Hiroshima and Nagasaki, and their impact on individuals, families, communities, the country, and the world community.

The authors I have quoted throughout this book, whose writings have greatly informed and influenced my work.

The many Rwandan children and young adults who continue to teach me so much about the extraordinary evil adults can inflict on the most vulnerable, for your resiliency and your determination to make real "never again."

Anna, Maria, and Joseph, for your love, encouragement, and daily presence through your calls, e-mails, and quick visits, but most of all for your readiness to open our home and your hearts to young people half a world away.

Don, for once again finding articles and books that either support or refute my writings, for being there with your lighthearted humor when our kids thought I might be "going over the edge," and for taking the enormity of this topic and bringing it into the here and now in our state of Colorado as you passionately fight for the rights of immigrants.

You, the reader. By purchasing this book you have made the life of a child in Rwanda a little bit better. Thank you for recognizing that "it does matter."

Credits

Index